TRAUMA HEALING

Advanced Workshop Manual

Nadine Hoover
Alternatives to Violence Project Facilitator

In collaboration with:

Lee Norton
Trauma Therapist

Pamela Haines
Co-Counseling Trainer

Copyright © 2010
Conscience Studio

90 W. University St., Alfred, New York 14802
www.ConscienceStudio.com

All rights reserved under International and Pan American Copyright Conventions. No part of this book may be reproduced in any form by any electronic or mechanical means, including information storage and retrieval systems, without permission in writing from the publisher.

Alternatives to Violence Project facilitators who serve as a volunteer to facilitate workshops in prisons or communities are granted the right to reproduce small quantities of this manual for non-commercial use without prior permission.

Hoover, Nadine with Lee Norton and Pamela Haines
   Trauma Healing: Advanced Workshop Manual

ISBN 978-0-9828492-0-0

1. Trauma Recovery
2. Counseling
3. Nonviolence
4. Self-Help

Cover Design: Terese Longva
Cover Photo: Olav Skarstein
Technical Support: Devin Henry

Photos: Greeting, Abyssinia Hoover by Terese Longva; Safety, Marilyn Showers and Dean Hoover by Terese Longva; Remembering, Cindy York and Sarah Rozard by Terese Longva; Mourning, Orchid by Autumn Star; Reconnecting, Anna Morales by Jenna Morales; Wrapping Up, Alternatives to Violence Project participants from East Aceh, Tamiang, North Sumatra and western New York State by Nadine Hoover.

Appreciation to Dr. Francine Shapiro for permission to reprint the VoC Scale.

Manufactured by Lightning Source, USA, UK and Australia.

*To Fenna and Sarah,
who have taken
this journey
with me.*

Table of Contents

Note to Readers — vii
Note to Facilitators — viii
Acknowledgements — ix

Workshop Routines

Schedule — 3
Agenda — 4
Gatherings — 6
Agenda Previews and Open Questions — 7
Light and Livelies — 8
Evaluations and Closings — 9
Materials List — 10

Workshop Sessions

GREETING: SESSION I — 13
Opening Talk — 14
Cooperative Agreement — 16
Step Into the Circle — 18
Stand on a Line — 20
Good Listening — 22
Listening Companions — 24
    A Good Listening Companion — 26
    Physical Discharge of Emotional Stress — 27
Companions: Ways I Receive Help — 28

SAFETY: SESSION II — 31
Stress and Reactions/SUDS — 32
Companions: Discharge — 35
Grounding: In This Chair — 36
Safe Place — 37
Transforming Power — 40
Concentric Circles — 41
Closing: Breathing — 43

REMEMBERING: SESSION III	45
Empty Chair	46
Grounding: One Object	46
Loss, Grief and Mourning	47
Light & Lively: Turn Up the Volume	47
Variation: Experiences of Grief	48
Stories of Trauma	49
MOURNING: SESSION IV	53
Positive Moments Sculpture	54
River of Life	55
RECONNECTING: SESSION V	57
Speak Out	58
Tree of Trust	60
WRAPPING UP: SESSION VI	61
Whisper Circle	62
Tracking and Balancing	63

Appendices

Appendix I: Companion Sessions	67
Appendix II: Grounding Techniques	69
Appendix III: Self Care and Soothing	72
Appendix IV: Questions and Answers	75

Handouts

Handout: The Subjective Units of Distress (SUD) Scale	85
Handout: Tracking How I Feel	86
Handout: Balancing How I Feel	87
Handout: Validity of Cognition (VoC) Scale	88
Handout: Workshop Evaluation Report (AVP-NY)	89
Handout: Readings and Resources	90

Note to Readers

This Manual is designed for the Alternatives to Violence Project (AVP), which has conducted three-day basic, advanced and training for facilitator workshops since 1975. AVP spread from New York to the United States to the world (see page 90, Readings and Resources). To become an AVP facilitator, one attends a basic workshop, an advanced workshop and a training for facilitators, and then apprentices on a team with experienced facilitators until recognized as a facilitator. An AVP facilitator must not only know how to facilitate the wide range of activities that form the workshop, but also grow in our own personal practice of living nonviolently day-to-day and be able to create trusting communities.

The reader is asked to participate in an Alternatives to Violence Project Basic workshop before participating in this workshop and, regardless of your background, to be a participant in this workshop before facilitating it. AVP workshops aren't to be conducted by just reading the manual.

As is the policy of the Alternatives to Violence Project, this workshop is facilitated by a team of three or more AVP facilitators, who are not paid but freely give their time. Facilitating this workshop creates the space for personal practice of health and wellbeing critical to a nonviolent life, as opposed to trying to fix or teach others.

Participants need to be stable in their lives. This is an opportunity to learn about trauma and healing techniques. Although participants find this workshop therapeutic, it is NOT designed to provide individual attention necessary for personal therapy. If at any time someone does not seem stable, be sure to refer him or her to an individualized support or care.

No participant may be in an institutional position of power over another participant—guard, teacher, administrator, etc. Family members need to realistically consider whether or not to participate in the same workshop. A team member needs speak with the youngest family member first to ensure there's no coercion, that he or she really wants to be there and feels free to be himself or herself with other family members present.

Note to Facilitators

As an Alternatives to Violence Project workshop, please be sure that:

1. The facilitator leading the workshop has taken the workshop.

2. A trauma therapist, trusted by the team, facilitates, consults or is available.

3. A list of therapeutic resources in the area is available including name and contact information for therapists, Re-evaluation Counseling communities, faith communities, spiritual counselors, spiritual friendships, Quaker meetings, 12-Step Programs and so forth.

4. The facilitation team has at least three to five members.

5. Team building, materials preparation and practice time are scheduled and completed prior to greeting participants for the workshop.

6. Team clinics are scheduled and convened on breaks during the workshop and immediately after the workshop, with an agenda that includes: check in; review evaluations; attend to participants; give and receive feedback; prepare next two agendas; and give and receive affirmations.

7. Workshop reports are written and sent to your local Alternatives to Violence Project office and/or AVP-USA, including number and names of each facilitator and each participant, time, place, schedule, agenda and any comments about the workshop.

8. Gatherings, groundings, companion sessions and self care are selected by the facilitation team in relation to the needs of the group. The specifics for time and activities in this agenda are merely suggestions.

Any part or the entire workshop may be used in other settings or for compensation as long as you use another name besides AVP, as doing so, although valid in itself, changes the fundamental nature of the time and work together and does not represent the Alternatives to Violence Project.

Acknowledgements

This manual combines insights from three lifetimes—Nadine Hoover, an Alternatives to Violence Project (AVP) facilitator in Alfred, NY; Lee Norton, a trauma therapist in Nashville, TN; and Pamela Haines, a Re-evaluation Co-counselor in Philadelphia, PA—informed by generations of dedicated people who taught us: Stephen Angell, Victoria Cooley, Harvey Jackins, Chuck Esser, Louis Tinnin MD and Linda Gantt PhD among others.

This manual would not exist without the honesty and courage to learn, change and do the right thing in the face of all odds of so many Indonesians in Aceh and North Sumatra, or without the knowledge, insight and generosity of the collaborators and AVP facilitators who volunteered long hours, particularly G. Mislan, Petrus, M. Dahlan, Ferrizal, and Ririn. Ririn gave patient, persistent attention to writing the first version in Indonesian while pilot testing with Acehnese, displaced Javanese and North Sumatrans through Friend Peace Teams to Indonesia.

Cecelia Yocum, trauma therapist in Tampa FL, working with Val Liveoak through Peacebuilding *en las Américas* of Friends Peace Teams contributed many activities, as did Carolyn Keys and many Africans who developed Healing and Rebuilding Our Communities (HROC) workshops conducted by the African Great Lakes Initiative of Friends Peace Teams.

One should never underestimate the support of people close to us—my two daughters, Fenna Mandolang and Sarah Rozard, each of whom in their own way cheered me on and tolerated my absence; my parents, Dean and Sharon Hoover, who always asked "Are you writing?"; my brother Mark Hoover Thames and his wife, Viticia Thames, who are always there for me; Kathleen Gale, David Snaith, Donna Starr, Autumn and Katy Star and Steve, Bronwyn, Alma and Elsa Mohlke who so generously offered hospitality; two dozen spiritual companions who tell me the truth; Karen Reixach and Sharon Hoover who edited the manuscript; Allen Grove who encouraged quality in publishing; AVP facilitators near and far who committed to practicing peace; and Jeanne Hyland, whose pure soul shines everyday and perpetually reminds us of life's preciousness.

We are grateful for the financial support of the Alternatives to Violence-New York, Farmington-Scipio Regional Meeting and New York Yearly Meeting of the Religious Society of Friends (Quakers) and donors to Friends Peace Teams to Indonesia, who invested in the development of this work that made this workshop a reality.

Workshop Routines

Schedule

This workshop agenda will take more than the eighteen hours outlined below, so the team must make choices among these recommended activities, particularly in the last half of the workshop or add another afternoon session to allow for all the activities. To do all these activities may require 21 to 28 hours in workshop sessions. In some communities, we add another full day to the schedule below.

An eighteen-hour schedule is typical for a weekend workshop and the minimum recommended, because it takes time to create community; to see one's self and others learn and change; and to absorb new ideas and behaviors. Workshops conducted in prison must adjust to the institution's particular scheduling constraints and religious communities must adjust to prayer and worship schedules for their faith and time zone.

Day 1	6:30 – 9:30	3 hrs	Session I:	Greeting
Day 2	8:30 – 11:30	3 hrs	Session II:	Safety
	1:00 – 3:00	2 hrs	Session III:	Remembering
	3:30 – 5:30	2 hrs	Session III:	Remembering
	6:30 – 9:30	3 hrs	Session IV:	Mourning
Day 3	8:30 – 11:30	3 hrs	Session V:	Reconnecting
	1:00 – 3:00	2 hrs	Session VI:	Wrapping Up
TOTAL	(minimum!)	18 hrs		

If you need to rearrange the schedule, be mindful of the activities. Do not schedule stories of violence and trauma right before bedtime or when people are not able to complete a whole activity.

Residential workshops are the best to give people time to interact outside of sessions and to ensure that the group stays consistent over the days and benefits from cooperative preparation, cooking and cleaning. For the workshop to be successful, rest times and spaces must be protected. Ask people to help, but also to take care of their own neeeds to stay healthy and rested.

Agenda

Greeting: Session I
Welcome and Agenda Preview
Gathering: Name and *what my adjective name means to me is*….
Opening Talk
Cooperative Agreement
Step Into the Circle
Light & Lively: Send a Goofy Face
Stand on a Line
Good Listening
Listening Companions
Companions: Ways I Receive Help…
Evaluation
Closing

Safety: Session II
Gathering: Name and *a time I listened to someone else was*….
Agenda Preview
Stress and Reactions/SUDS
Companions: Discharge
Grounding: In this Chair
Light & Lively: Here I Sit
Safe Place
Transforming Power
Concentric Circles
Closing

Remembering: Session III
Gathering: Name and *one person who loves me is*….
Agenda Preview
Empty Chair
Grounding: One Object
Light & Lively: Sounding Circle
Loss, Grief and Mourning
Light & Lively: Turn Up the Volume
Self Care: Breathing
Stories of Trauma

Mourning: Session IV
Gathering: Name and *two words for how I feel right now are*....
Agenda Preview
Positive Moments Sculpture
Companions: A Good Companion
Self Care: Massage
Light & Lively: Wake Up in the Forest
River of Life
Grounding: Fingers
Evaluation of the Day
Closing

Reconnecting: Session V
Gathering: Name and *one person I trust and why*....
Agenda Preview
Companions: Trust and Mistrust
Grounding: 3, 2, 1
Shout Out
Light & Lively: Elephant, Bird, Palm Tree
Tree of Trust
Self Care: Self Soothing
Check-In

Wrapping Up: Session VI
Gathering: Name and *one thing I'll take home with me is*....
Agenda Preview
Whisper Circle
Tracking and Balancing
Grounding: Pleasant Memories
Open Questions
Next Steps
Evaluation
Closing: Goodbye Circle

Gatherings

Purposes
To gather a sense of group at the beginning of a session, learn from each other, prepare for central activities, give participants an opportunity to speak, shift power to all participants equally and honor the rule to respect self and others. Often after we have a chance to speak and be heard, we are more available to pay attention to others.

Time
10-20 minutes (highly dependent on how the facilitator models the activity and how many people are in the group).

Materials
Places for all participants (including facilitators) to sit in a circle, preferably with no obstructions in the center of the circle between people, so everyone has a clear line of sight to everyone else.

Instructions
The facilitation team picks sentences or questions for the gathering and writes them on the agenda posted on the wall so everyone can see. You may use the suggested ones or pick others that fit the group, the theme, the work of the session and the time available.

When everyone is seated, you may say, *"Welcome. We're ready to start our gathering."* Don't add more words than this at the beginning. Don't say lots of different things or make jokes, just say this simply and preserve as much time as possible for others to speak. The facilitators all think of at least one example of a response and practice it with another facilitator. *"My name is _____; and…"* read the question or sentence off the agenda, looking and even pointing to it so others get oriented to where it is on the wall, but do not leave your seat. Try to be succinct, concrete and personal. If you ramble on, seem unsure, or are vague, others will follow your example. We do not typically debrief Gatherings.

Agenda Previews

Purposes
To share the power and information and to give participants a sense of where the session is going.

Time
Three to five minutes.

Materials
Agenda written and posted on the wall. The agenda must be big enough to be seen around the room, typically use half a sheet of flip chart paper or a white board or chalk board to save trees and funds.

Instructions
A facilitator stands next to the agenda posted on the wall, turns to face the group and points to the agenda on his or her side. The facilitator reads each item on the agenda as it is, slowly and with pauses between activities. The facilitator pauses after reading all of them, then sits down in the circle.

Open Questions

Purposes: To honor everyone's learning process and the group's time. To give individuals time to find their own answers through the activities.

Time: 1-2 minutes in Opening Talk and 5-60 minutes in last session.
Materials: Sheet with a sheet titled Open Questions posted and a marker.

Instructions: Follow instructions in the Opening Talk. In the last session of the workshop, Open Questions may be combined with Next Steps. A set of great questions may require up to an hour of discussion. Invite discussion among the whole group; don't try to give lengthy expert answers. If participants have specialized questions or seek expert advice, consider scheduling a talk by an expert or referring people to readings.

Light and Livelies

Purposes: To keep people awake, activate their cerebral cortex, bring them fully into present time, teach lessons in a kinesthetic manner, modulate emotion, relax and enjoy one's self, others and life!

Time: 10-30 minutes depending on the activity.

Materials: None.

Instructions: These activities should be familiar to Alternatives to Violence Project facilitators. "Turn Up the Volume" is not from AVP, so it is described as an activity. As is our custom, these Light and Livelies are just suggestions; if you choose replacements or additions, be sure they are consistent with the roadmap for the Alternatives to Violence Project and trauma healing.

Send a Goofy Face: Turn to your left or right and make a goofy face. Your neighbor looks at you and copies it. He or she then makes a different goofy face to the next person, who copies it and turns to the next person and so forth.

Here I Sit: One chair is vacant. Whomever to the right or left gets into the chair first, says, "Here I sit." The next person moves one chair over and says, "In this chair." The next person moves one chair over and says, "With my friend, …" and adds the adjective name of someone in the group. The person named runs across the circle to sit in the vacant chair and the process repeats.

Wake Up in the Forest: Around the circle have each person say their adjective name, an animal and make the sound. Then everyone crouches down, starting with a quiet voice and getting louder as the group stands.

Elephant, Bird, Palm Tree: A person in the center of the circle points to someone and says either elephant, bird or palm tree, who must work with both his or her neighbors to make it. Bird with beak at mouth and wings. Palm with fronds going up and out. Elephant with trunk and two ears.

Evaluations

Purposes: To allow time for recall to reinforce learning. To give participants power to say whatever they want or need to say without comment, rebuttal or interruption. To give facilitators feedback and a sense of the group.

Time: 10-15 minutes.

Materials: Agenda posted visibly, a sheet with columns for "+," "–" and "light bulb" posted and a dark marker. Other materials if varying approach.

Instructions: Review the agenda with enough time and reference for people's minds physically to remember what happened; you will see it in their face and eyes when they catch a real memory of each moment. After that, either ask what they liked, didn't like or if they have any suggestions, or ask: *"What did you get out of this session? Was it worth your time to do this? Do you understand* [session theme] *better?"* After some time to comment, add: *"What didn't work? What do you need?"* Face the participants and let another facilitator write. Don't turn your back on the participants or comment. Facilitators DO NOT participate in evaluations. Write the participants' words; do not reinterpret or "improve" on what they say. Thank them.

Closings

Purposes: To bring the group together, acknowledging that we are all doing this together as well as doing our work individually. To create an orderly transition, letting go of what we have been doing and preparing to move on to other activities. To affirm the work and commitment to take this work into our day-to-day lives and interactions with others and the world.

Time: 5-10 minutes.

Materials and Instructions: Depends on the closing used, see your Alternatives to Violence Project Basic manual for suggestions, materials and instructions.

Materials List

Materials:
Markers & 25-40 flip chart sheets (fewer if using half sheets when possible)
Masking tape with place to hang and write on posters
Drawing paper 8 ½" x 11", twelve for each person
Large drawing paper 11" x 17", one for each person
Notecards 3" x 5", one for each person
Drawing: crayons, markers, colored pencils, oil pastels, whatever you have
Pens and pencils for each person
Boxes of tissues
Journal/blank book for each person (optional)
Transforming Power Cards and Mandala
Grief Cards (optional)
Tree trunk and branches drawn and cut to post on wall
Leaves, fruit and roots for each person (twice as many leaves if you'd like)
Gong (optional)

Posters:
Opening Talk; Purposes of this Workshop; Trauma Healing Roadmap; Cooperative Agreement; A Good Listening Companion; Physical Discharge of Emotional Stress; Definition of Trauma; SUD Scale; Loss; Grief; Mourning; Tell About One Situation; Complete These Sentences; Secondary Trauma

Titles:
Group Contract; Ways I Take Care of Myself; Good Listening; Poor Listening; Open Questions; Regular Stress; Traumatic Stress; Reactions to Trauma; Safety; Times We're Bystanders to Violence; How it Feels to be Bystanders to Violence; Ways to Respond as Bystanders to Violence

Handouts:
SUD Scale (one for each person)
VoC (one for each person)
Tracking How I Feel (one for each person or booklet made)
Balancing How I Feel (one for each person or booklet made)
Copies of **TRAUMA HEALING**: *Advanced Workshop Manual*
Resources Available for Follow-Up (make your own for your area)

Workshop Sessions

GREETING: SESSION I

Welcome
Agenda Preview
Gathering: Name and *what my positive adjective name means to me is....*
or *what I hope from this workshop is....*
or *what I'd be doing if I weren't here is....*
Opening Talk
Cooperative Agreement
Step Into the Circle
Light & Lively: Send a Goofy Face
Stand on a Line
Good Listening
Listening Companions
Companions: Ways I Receive Help...
Evaluation
Closing

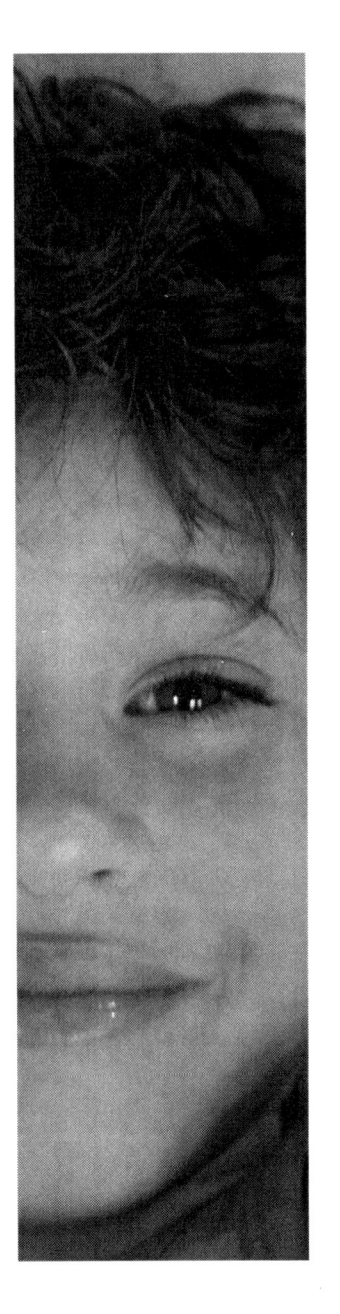

Opening Talk

"This is an Alternatives to Violence Project (AVP) advanced workshop using the AVP philosophy and approach based on being open to transforming power from within and beyond, a palpable power in the world available to each of us to change ourselves, others and situations for the better. We have all made a commitment to practice nonviolence in our daily lives and are each here as a volunteer, attending with no pay as participants or facilitators.

"This is an experiential workshop where learning grows from experiences and reflections on experiences to create insight, rather than on experts or lectures, and is reinforced by recalling each session at the end of the session or day. For trauma healing, however, we do not support experiential 're-living' of a traumatic event. The work of remembering is: 1) balanced by the presence of a companion to draw one's attention to the present while remembering the past; 2) modulated by breaking it up into small sections and 3) processed into narrative through art, analysis and retelling. Tempered with precautions, remembering may decrease rigidity, distress patterns and reenactment. Experiential dramatization or acting out of past traumatic events without a companion or without reprocessing can increase rather than decrease distress and should be avoided.

"This workshop organizes activities drawn from:
1. A new generation of trauma healing methods based on brain research, which attend to safety, remembering, mourning and reconnection.
2. Re-evaluation Counseling or Co-counseling for how to be a listening companion to someone reprocessing and healing from traumatic experiences.
3. Alternatives to Violence Project (AVP) on practicing nonviolence in prisons, community, and, through Friends Peace Teams, in former war zones, realizing the great need for trauma healing for victims and perpetrators alike."

Have multiple boxes of tissues available and post on the wall two sheets:

> **Purposes of this Workshop**
> Gain an understanding of trauma.
> Learn tools to create safe space and face traumatic events.
> Rebuild social relationships and trust.
> Learn to be a companion to others healing from trauma.

> **Trauma Healing Road Map**
> Be safe with self and others – Affirmation
> Remember and mourn losses – Communication
> Reconnect and rebuild trust – Cooperation
> Use transforming power to face and resolve conflicts

"This workshop is a place to learn the language of and methods for healing from difficult incidents in one's own history. It is NOT personal therapy, but may provide therapeutic tools or approaches that participants can use in other contexts. In order to learn, we need to feel safe. If you abuse alcohol or drugs, feel suicidal, go out looking for fights, or are being put down, abused or attacked at work, at home or in the community, then you need individualized support to remedy that first. This is not a good time to participate in this workshop. We ask that all participants are sober for thirty days prior to taking this workshop. If you are currently living under any of these conditions, please speak to one of the facilitators after this session.

"Are there any questions or comments at this point?" Pause. *"As we go through the workshop, if you have any questions or comments please speak up. There is also a paper posted here on the wall for "Open Questions." Anytime a question arises that we cannot address at the time, or on a break, feel free to write your questions here. Sometimes we may suggest that rather than answering a question, we can put it on the Open Questions sheet to respond to later or at the end of the workshop."*

Cover any logistics that are needed to support the workshop, such as:
1. *"To take photos, please let us know and we'll ask the group for permission."*
2. *"Who's going to write a report for this workshop to send to AVP?"*
3. *"Please explain the logistics so everyone will be comfortable while we're here: bathrooms, telephones, meal arrangements, sleeping arrangements, clean-up, etc...."*
4. *"Does anyone have anything to add? Does anyone have any questions?"*

It's nice for a facilitator to know what to say briefly and clearly. Do not follow this script word-for-word, put it into your own words but do not add lots of words or tangents. Say as little as possible while getting the ideas and information across. This is not a test. If you prefer to refer to notes, that's okay. Just don't read from them or from the manual. Leave the manual outside the circle and speak directly to the group.

Cooperative Agreement

Purposes
To introduce a set of essential ground rules. To develop a common language and understanding of the rules and their applications. To provide space for participants to express themselves, seek clarification, share ideas and perspectives, question the facilitators, exercise power, negotiate with facilitators and experience agreement among all present. To honor and balance the power of both participants and facilitators by explicitly and mutually coming to agreement on a common set of rules for behavior. To solicit everyone's participation in reminding and enforcing the agreement.

Time: 30 minutes or more.

Materials: The list of agreements and a blank sheet posted on the wall.

Cooperative Agreement

Affirm self and others; no put downs

Listen; don't interrupt

Participate; Keep it short and simple

Ask for help and help others

Speak from one's own experience

Share your own story; not others'

Volunteer one's self only

Everyone has the right to pass and to privacy

Take care of yourself and the group

Instructions
Tell participants we find this workshop works if we all understand and agree to this set of agreements. It's important that everyone understand each of these. Read the cooperative agreement one by one slowly. Then ask if there are any questions? Turn to the whole group to see if other facilitators [pause] or participants want to respond or comment. Edit and/ or add whatever is needed to establish a mutual understanding of and

appreciation for these rules. If at all possible make additions or edits using the participants' words to honor their effort to process and integrate these ideas, as long as no substance is lost. If people do not agree, spend the time at the beginning to come to an understanding that everyone can accept. Remember discussion at this point may have as much or more to do with negotiating power as negotiating understanding, so here is the facilitators' real life test on how well and graciously they share power and at the same time can be trusted to maintain the content and the "container."

Ask if everyone understands all the points. Ask if everyone agrees to follow them all for the duration of the workshop, inside and outside the sessions. Make eye contact with every participant and confirm a positive gesture or response from every participant. Silence is not considered agreement.

Ask if any other guidelines are needed for us to feel safe and do our best work. Begin by listening to the group and writing their words and language on the paper or board posted. After three or more participants have spoken, facilitators may add things, too.

On a blank sheet on the wall under the Cooperative Agreement, fill in additional items such as:
- Say your adjective name before speaking.
- Don't bring up other people's stories outside the session.
- Turn cell phones to silent or off.
- Be on time, sitting in the session before the appointed hour.
- Everyone participates in the work of food preparation and clean up.
- No smoking during sessions or inside the room or building.
- Break for prayer times or church services.
- Use hand signals at appropriate times.
- Take care of yourself quietly, quickly, without disrupting your group.
- No side discussions in the large group.
- Be sure to go to sleep, so all are rested for the next day.
- If you have to leave the circle, tell a facilitator why.

We typically do not debrief the Cooperative Agreement, but you may.

Note: Use the language of these agreements frequently and draw people's attention back to them regularly as you go through the workshop.

Step into the Circle

Purposes
To get to know people and find similarities among us. Depending on the group, more difficult questions may form bonds in the group and build a sense of safety in sharing difficult things about ones' self early in the workshop, noting our similarities and differences, but this must be done gently. Opening up too early too deeply may create a sense of isolation, distrust and need for protection. Working with people you work with regularly over time is different than people you don't see regularly.

Time
20 minutes.

Materials
List of questions (held by the facilitator).

Instructions
Ask everyone to stand in a circle. You may play a few rounds of Big Wind Blows to mix up the group. Then, explain: *"In this activity we give several examples of questions to get to know each other and if that is true for you, then you step into the circle. The group will be quiet a moment and imagine what life is like for those for whom it is true and for those for whom it is not true. After facilitators give a few examples, anyone may call out, 'Step into the circle if you....'"* Then, ask facilitators: *"Do you have anything to add?"* Ask participants: *"Any questions?"*

Examples of questions are:
"Please step in the circle if you…"
- …have children.
- …like _____.
- …have traveled to _____.

Let others ask "get to know you" questions after you model a couple examples.

If a discussion emerges from a question or position, let the discussion happen naturally, while still being mindful of the time needed to finish the activity.

If you feel the group can handle more challenges, you may ask:

- …*have hurt another person?*
- …*faced violence in your own family?*
- …*are scared of sleeping at night?*
- …*isolate yourself?* …*feel abandoned?*
- …*were shot at?* …*carried a weapon?*
- …*hurt yourself, including drinking, drugging or looking for fights?*
- …*have ever given up on life or felt suicidal?*
- …*wanted revenge or got revenge?*

- …*felt listened to and understood by someone else?*
- …*felt someone else helped you?*
- …*felt loved by someone else?*
- …*felt you are more than enough?*
- …*feel accepted just as you are?*
- …*feel smart and capable?*
- …*know how to take care of yourself?*
- …*love yourself and others?*
- …*trust someone else?*
- …*feel beautiful or handsome?*
- …*felt listened to with love?*
- …*are a good parent or had good parents?*

Debriefing
What did you notice from doing this?
What did it feel like to do this activity?
What new learning did you get from doing this?
What will you take home and do differently because of this?
How is this related to healing from trauma and living nonviolently?

Stand on a Line

Purposes
To be more conscious of how we take care of ourselves. To share ideas for taking better care of ourselves, especially at times of stress.

Time
30 minutes.

Materials
Paper on the wall titled "Ways I Take Care of Myself" and markers.

Instructions
Begin by remembering the road map for trauma healing: safety, remembering and reconnecting. The first step is to be safe with one's self and others. Then brainstorm: "Ways I take care of myself." For example:
- Rest and sleep regularly and enough
- Exercise, walk, move my body
- Use personal and family money carefully and wisely
- Pray, meditate
- Bathe, care for personal hygiene
- Take care of my health (seek traditional or medical attention)
- Be neat and keep my house neat
- Go out to social events
- Eat regularly
- Take time to relax alone
- Do not use drugs, alcohol, etc…
- Open conversation with a friend
- Have a clear, personal goal
- Trust myself

Facilitators may add items AFTER participants have given a number of their own. After the brainstorm, have everyone stand up. Point to one wall that represents zero percent, none, never, not at all and the opposite wall that represents one hundred percent, all the time, completely. Note that each person can stand anywhere on that line—half way, most of the time, not too much, a little bit, etc.… Stand on the line and move your body along the line accordingly as you speak to represent what you are saying. If time is limited, simply ask: *"How well do you take care of yourself?"* Then interview people along the line about why they stood where they did. If time permits, ask about individual items from the brainstorm.

Say to the group, while pointing in the corresponding direction: *"When I read a question, if you never do this stand by that wall, if you always do it stand by that wall. Or choose anywhere in between."* After giving the instructions and possibly trying one example, ask: *"Do you have anything to add? Any questions?"*

- *"How much do you* [insert item from brainstorm]?" Invite everyone to look at where they and others stand and think about it for a moment.
- Then ask: *"Where do you wish you were actually standing? Don't move, just look and think about it first."* ... (give a moment)... *"Now move to the place where you wish you were standing."* Give them a minute in the new place.
- Then ask: *"What would you need to do to be able to go from where you were first standing to where you are standing now? What concretely would have to change? What would you have to do in your life?"* Encourage them to speak.

Debriefing
What did you notice from doing this?
What did it feel like to do this activity?
What new learning did you get from doing this?
What will you take home and do differently because of this?
How is this related to healing from trauma and living nonviolently?

Good Listening

Purpose
To identify skills used in effective listening so we can practice throughout the workshop and beyond, which may avert or resolve misunderstandings or conflicts and which may contribute to positive relationships and caring.

Time
5 – 15 minutes (some facilitators have longer approaches, but it's helpful to conserve time here and there will be lots of opportunity to practice).

Materials
Paper for brainstorm divided in two: "Good Listening" "Poor Listening."

Instructions
Conduct a brainstorm on "What is Good Listening" followed by "What is Poor Listening." Always let participants give the first three to five items, then facilitators can participate as well. Facilitators ensure the following items are included:

Good Listening	Poor Listening
Maintain Eye Contact	Interrupt
Look Interested-Be Interested	Give Advice
Be Aware of What Is Said	Tell a Better Story
Notice What is Not Said	Judge
Question to Clarify Only	Express Your Opinions

After the brainstorm, tell people: *"Eighty percent of communication is nonverbal. Show me with your bodies what is good listening."* Pause. *"Oh, that is better!"* [Pause.] *"What do you feel or notice about good listening? What do you notice about the things on the board?"* Look back at the brainstorm results. *"With your bodies, show me poor listening."* Pause, model what you are looking for with your own body. *"Okay. Show me* [insert a type of listening here].*"*

Types of Listening
Bored Listening
Anxious Listening
Distracted Listening
Relaxed Listening
Engaged Listening—I can't wait to hear the end of this!
Want-to-Listen-but-I'm-Falling-Asleep Listening
Want-to-Listen-but-Need-to-Go Listening
Don't-Want-to-Listen-and-Need-to-Go Listening
Angry Listening —YEAH, YEAH I'M LISTENING!
Horrified Listening
I Wanna Talk Too Listening
Interested, Engaged, Non-anxious Listening

Make up your own types of listening. A few examples suffice. Don't get carried away. Use the ways you've noticed individuals in the group listen or not listen to others.

Tell people: *"There's a lot going on inside the listener and whatever is going on inside the listener affects the speaker. These are general guidelines, but nonverbal communication is different for each person, culture and situation."* End with the interested, engaged, non-anxious listening. Note to the group that this is the type of listening we want.

Debriefing
What did you notice about yourself doing this?
What makes you comfortable or uncomfortable when someone is listening to you?
What makes you comfortable or uncomfortable when you are listening to someone else?
How does the nonverbal communication of listening open us to transforming power?
How might effective listening help in a conflict situation at home or at work?

Listening Companions

Purposes
To learn ways to be present with someone while she is remembering difficult times in ways that help heal rather than increase problems.

Time
40 minutes.

Materials
Posters of "A Good Listening Companion," "Physical Discharge of Emotional Stress," "SUD Scale" and "Resources Available for Follow-Up."

Instructions
"In this workshop, we will practice being companions to each other while taking turns practicing techniques to remember difficult incidents in a way that isn't just reliving the trauma, but allows for mourning and reconnection." Have different participants read one item each from "Good Listening Companion" poster slowly so people may digest the new ideas.

"Do you understand this? Are there any questions of clarification at this point?" Give a long pause. *"How do you feel about these directions? Do you think you could follow them when listening to someone else? Are you willing to practice in this workshop?"* Allow for some reflection, exchange and discussion. *"If there's one that will be hard for you, let's talk about it now, because we are hoping that everyone will agree to practice all of these while we are here together."* Again, leave long pauses and encourage discussion. *"Can we all agree to this?"* Make eye contact with each participant to solicit an active verbal or nonverbal affirmation.

"It is helpful to have an understanding of the physical discharge of emotional stress in order to do this work well." Have different participants read one item each from the "Physical Discharge of Emotional Stress" poster slowly so people may digest the new ideas.

Explain, *"SUDS is a scale from one, no stress at all, to ten, maximum emotional distress. We would like to stay at a 3-5 level. If you feel your speaking partner is going above or below this, as a partner you may ask, 'Where are you on the SUD Scale?' or 'Where is your distress from one to ten?' Even if you feel you are not good with numbers, please try to use this during this workshop. To control your level of distress stop, calm down, use grounding techniques, ask for help, then proceed OR challenge your self to dig deeper or take a risk to pay attention to more distressing parts of your life."* Pause. Look at the facilitators. *"Is there anything to add?"* Look at everyone. *"Are there any questions?"*

Explain, *"We recommend follow up to this workshop. You may:*
- *Continue meeting regularly with your listening companion or other person every one, two, three, four or six weeks or once or twice a month.*
- *Establish a spiritual friendship, possibly from within your religious group.*
- *Explore the Re-evaluation Counseling community to see what they have available.*
- *Participate in 12-Step Programs with a sponsor.*
- *Begin working regularly with a local trauma therapist or counselor."*

A GOOD LISTENING COMPANION

Listen from the heart with courtesy, full attention and relaxed concern, showing confidence in another's goodness and capabilities.

Stay grounded in the present, call the other's attention enough to the present and to your connection to balance attention between the past and present, between what's going on inside and outside.

Understand that a non-anxious presence helps one persist in repeated recountings and that loss of language and avoidance are natural reactions to trauma.

Follow the person's choice of what to work on—specific experiences or telling one's life story may reveal tender topics that could receive more attention.

Ask questions to show interest; encourage someone to talk about self, difficult experiences and distress patterns; or direct attention to emotionally charged material.

Encourage physical release of emotion and attend to where release occurs, while showing confidence in the person's ability to stay enough in the present to allow learning to occur.

Take turns of equal time being a listening companion and being listened to; study and practice being counseled as well as counseling.

DO NOT
LET ANOTHER PERSON'S TROUBLES BOTHER YOU!
Interrupt or pursue your own curiosity.
Tell similar problems you've had in the past.
Give advice, suggestions or answers to problems.
React emotionally or over-sympathize, stealing others' emotions.

PHYSICAL DISCHARGE OF EMOTIONAL STRESS

Emotional Stress	Physical Release
Grief	➤ Tears, crying, sobbing
Heavy Fears	➤ Trembling, shivering, cold sweat, urinating
Light Fears/Embarrassment	➤ Laughter, cold sweat
Heavy Angers	➤ Angry noise, violent movement, warm sweat
Light Angers	➤ Laughter, warm sweat
Physical Pains/Tension	➤ Yawns, stretching, scratching
Boredom	➤ Nonrepetitive conversing, laughing

Emotional stress is released naturally from the body as a sign of healing, not hurt.

With a listening companion's help, practice encouraging and not interrupting your own talking or physical release of emotion, while you also:

- Balance remembering with being in a safe, affirming, non-anxious present.

- Keep distress levels **HIGH** enough to work—a one or two on a ten point scale may be too low to feel the work.

- Keep distress levels **LOW** enough to learn—over a five on a ten point scale may be too distracting to maintain the awareness necessary for learning.

- Maintain a sense of present time while you remember and return fully to the present time when you are finished remembering.

Companions: Ways I Receive Help

Purposes
To practice listening with interest and relaxed concern. To practice talking more deeply about personally difficult experiences and discharging the emotions associated with them. To practice ways of accompanying each other in the work of healing. For variations on Companions, see Appendix I: Companion Sessions, page 67.

Time
25-30 minutes.

Materials
Be sure "Physical Discharge of Emotional Stress" and "A Good Listening Companion" posters are visible on the wall.

Instructions
"Find a partner you live close to and may be able to meet again after this workshop if you choose to do so. For now, however, the only commitment is to support each other through the course of this workshop.

"Take a moment to look over the posters: 'Physical Discharge of Emotional Stress' and 'A Good Listening Companion.' Remember, this is what we are practicing.

"Be sure that both people get equal time—you must keep track of time when you are in a pair. When you meet, give the same number of minutes to the first person, switch at a given time and give the same number of minutes to the second person. Even if one or both are quiet for some time, be patient, give time for just thinking and reflecting and see if more comes. Take turns being the speaker and the listener and speak for three to five minutes on the topic. Say your name and talk about: 'Things other people do that make me feel helped and supported are....' or 'The best ways to help me are....'

"I will tell you when to begin and when to switch. After both persons have spoken, you will be given a few minutes (3-5 minutes) just to talk to each other about giving and receiving help from each other." Pause. Look at facilitators. *"Is there anything to add?"* Look at everyone. *"Are there any questions?"*

Debrief
What did it feel like to do this activity?
What did you get out of listening?
What did you get out of speaking?
What did you learn from doing this?
How is this related to healing and nonviolence?
What will you take home from this activity?

NOTE: The first time listening companions meet, the facilitator monitors time and tells participants when to switch speakers or to talk among themselves. Each time the listening companions meet, work towards the pairs managing their own time. Remember it is awkward for them at first. They will naturally want to violate the structure, so monitor their adherence to the time structure and gently remind them that this is a chance to practice something that is new and may not feel natural at the beginning, but eventually will feel quite natural, but only if they practice it with intent.

SAFETY: SESSION II

Gathering: Name and *a time I listened to someone else was*....
Agenda Preview
Stress and Reactions
Companions: Discharge
Grounding: In this Chair
Light & Lively: Here I Sit
Safe Place
Transforming Power
Concentric Circles
Closing

Stress and Reactions/SUDS

Purposes
To introduce the concepts of regular and traumatic stress and to be able to distinquish between them. To get to know different reactions to regular or traumatic stress. To see the relationship between traumatic incidents and reactions to them in daily life.

Time: One hour.

Materials: Definition of trauma and three posters on the wall: "Regular Stress," "Traumatic Stress" and "Reactions to Trauma," and the "SUD Scale" handout or poster.

Instructions
Brainstorm "Regular Stress" (running late, too much to do, good news, traffic, etc…) and "Traumatic Stress" (death, loss of ___, car accident, acts of war, torture, etc…). Give people time to look at both of the lists and discuss the differences. The facilitator may be very quiet and give people room to think and talk. Bring the focus back by slowly reading and considering this definition of trauma.

> **Definition of Trauma**
> Trauma is caused by events that overwhelm the ordinary adaptations to life. Traumatic events generally involve threats to life or bodily integrity, or a close personal encounter with violence or death. No instance is universally traumatic, so one can't judge the event alone. Trauma is a feeling that is so overwhelming that one is reduced to terror and helplessness.   Adapted from *Judith Herman, 1983*

Give people time to talk. When they're done, point out that: 1) regular stress and traumatic stress are a continuum from everyday occurrences to disasters, catastrophes and inhumane acts; 2) neither are something to be ashamed of; reacting to them is normal; and 3) no act is universally traumatic; we cannot judge trauma by the event, but rather by our reaction to the event.

If we feel ashamed, we close off and don't want to know, but if we are not ashamed we become curious, which opens the door to healing,

Remind participants, *"Traumatic incidents may reactivate rigid distress recordings. Please use the SUD Scale. If you feel your stress is going above a five, please let me know."* If someone lets you know, you may do a quick grounding technique with the individual or group, introduce grounding techniques early or narrate how distress patterns may be released or modulated through the series of discharge and grounding activities that follow.

Go to the third sheet, "Reactions to Trauma," and ask what reactions we have to traumatic stress. You may draw a line down the middle and write the causes of trauma on the left and reactions to it on the right, if these aren't naturally addressed. Or add appropriate items to the sheet on "Traumatic Stress." Brainstorm: *"What causes trauma? What types of incidents? What things can we see? Hear? Do? Experience? What reactions follow such incidents?"* Give people time to offer input, then add little by little any items that seem to be missing. The facilitators are responsible for making sure a variety of reactions are covered, such as:

- Felt shocked or frozen
- Couldn't breath
- Lost sensation in my body
- Followed orders; did what I was told
- Felt confused and sad
- Lost or have gaps in memory
- Frantic attachment to others, fear of abandonment
- Unstable sense of self or value of self
- Unstable relationships with others—idealizing and devaluing
- Impulsive in spending, sex, drugs, alcohol, driving or binge eating
- Hard to make decisions
- Lost appetite; not able to eat
- Eat all the time; can't stop
- Lack of personal hygiene
- Look for trouble/ look for a fight
- Flashbacks and nightmares
- Difficulty sleeping

- Tired, feeling lazy, not wanting to do anything
- Isolate and close one's self; don't want to speak
- Felt crazy
- Told the story over and over again to anyone who would listen
- Cried for justice
- Sought a way forward; wanted to figure it out and fix it
- Demanded public acknowledgement; wanted public witnesses
- Always remembering, memories come without control
- Crying; feel emotional all the time
- Paranoid, always on guard
- Avoid situations or people who trigger the memory
- Felt disconnected from others
- Lost self confidence
- Suspicious, afraid, anxious
- Distrust others
- Out of control anger
- Rage, hatred, want revenge
- Always feel wrong
- Always feel like I'm making mistakes
- Don't trust life
- Unstable; feel wild moodiness, or suicidal
- Self-mutilation
- Feel empty
- Feel like it could happen again at any time
- Can't think straight; feel confused
- Lost language and expression

Stand back, let people look at all three lists and talk as a group. No need to formally debrief; discussion usually ensues.

Note: The brainstorm should include some from each category of symptoms listed below. Some people like to post this; we typically do not.

> ### Categories of Symptoms of Trauma
> Intrusive symptoms, e.g. emotional or physical flashbacks, rage....
>
> Avoidance and loss of ability to feel emotion.
>
> Arousal, disruption of sleep or concentration, easily startled....
>
> Loss of a sense of meaning, sense of being lost, suicidal.

Companions: Discharge

Purposes
To practice listening with interest and relaxed concern. To practice talking more deeply about personally difficult experiences and discharging the emotions associated with them. To practice ways of accompanying each other in the work of healing.

Time: 20 minutes.

Materials: Spaces for pairs to get away from each other and focus.

Instructions
Invite everyone to get with the same companion they had before and find a place to themselves. After everyone is sitting in a pair, say: *"Please look back at the 'Physical Discharge of Emotional Stress.'"* Pause for time to read. *"Choose who will be the first person to speak and who will be the companion. Look over, 'A Good Listening Companion' and remember the goal of the companion is to listen with interest and relaxed concern so as to permit and encourage discharge, without being carried away with emotion one's self. The speaker takes five minutes to remember a problem or painful event and notices how the body responds, i.e. recall one of the saddest, scariest or most enraging times in your life and tries to enter into feeling it rather than just retelling it. What do you feel in your body? ...and where? What specific physical discharge do you feel well up? Don't inhibit discharge; allow it to occur. You may speak, but you do not have to. It helps to make noises that arise. Allow the discharge while you remember the event or problem. When it's time to switch, to come back to the present time the listening companion asks his or her partner, 'What color is my shirt?' or to describe something ordinary in the environment. Realize it's not easy, it's just an opportunity: 1) to notice the feeling of physical discharge in your body and then 2) to return to present time."* Pause. *"Is there anything to add?" "Are there any questions?"* If pairs go to private spaces, tell them to make sure each person takes five minutes with a couple minutes for grounding after each each person finishes. Go around and pay attention to all pairs.

Debrief
What did it feel like to do this activity? What did you learn from this activity? What will you take home from this? How is this related to healing and nonviolence?

Grounding: In This Chair

Purposes
To give short, simple, effective techniques to use when distress levels rise to the point that a person begins to get carried away with emotion, in other words when the person begins to "daydream," "fly," lose language or dissociate. To help a person come back to their senses and be grounded in the present. To increase a person's capabilities to bring themselves back to present time practicing techniques that are easy to use in any setting. For variations on Groundings, see Appendix II: Grounding Techniques, pg 69.

Time: 3-5 minutes.

Materials: None.

Instructions
"Groundings are techniques that help us come back to present time and place when distress takes us away. Now is a good time to do a grounding, since you just paid attention to something that was distressful. Ask your partner random questions, such as: 'What color is my shirt?' or 'What do you know about Norway?' Use groundings in the future after activities that trigger distress." Pause. Adjust the way you're sitting into a more relaxed manner.

"At this moment, you are very safe. Notice all the goodwill around you. We are now going to do a grounding called 'In This Chair.'" The repetition of the same words at the opening of every grounding may create a "voice" that comes when participants need it.

"Feel your bottom on your chair (or floor). Notice the legs of the chair go down to the floor. Notice the floor goes out to the walls and the walls go into the foundation of the building. Notice the foundation goes into the ground and the ground spreads out to be the town of [Name] *which is on the earth and the earth is a large ball of mass in the universe. The universe supports the earth, which supports the town of* [Name], *which supports this plot of ground, which supports the foundation of this building, which supports the walls, which supports the floor, which supports the chair, which supports me. I am supported by all of this."*

Safe Place

Purposes
To enable participants to imagine in specific detail a place where he or she feels safe. To have a safe place to go within one's self when one faces traumatic incidents.

Time
One hour and 15-30 minutes.

Materials
Poster on the wall titled "Safety," drawing paper for each person, crayons, colored pencils, and other coloring materials, an example of writing "[Name's] Safe Place" on a sheet of drawing paper.

Instructions
"It's best if we have some understanding of safety. We may know a lot about violence and danger, but how much do we know about and understand being safe? What do we imagine safety to be? Let's try to think concretely and in detail, not in generalizations. We will do a brainstorm of what conditions help you to feel safe."

If someone seems confused or seems to not feel they know the feeling of safety, ask them what it might be like if they did know or what would they imagine it to be like. After the brainstorm has been going on for awhile, interrupt the group and ask them to look back at the brainstorms on regular stress, traumatic stress and reactions to trauma. Remember stress is normal in everyday life. Look at traumatic stress and reactions to trauma. *"What if these did not exist? What would that be like?"* Return to the brainstorm on Safety. Some examples a facilitator might add towards the end if participants have not brought them up are:

Potential Brainstorm "Safety"

- Free to speak one's opinion
- Free from fear and hurt
- Calm in our hearts and minds
- Unguarded, open
- Justice is served
- Independent
- Healthy
- Lots of friends
- No prejudice
- Honest
- Satisfied with what we have
- Basic needs met
- Feel like eating
- Free to gather and meet
- Feel capable
- Be good to and like one's self
- Lots of colors
- Sincere
- Free to try out new things
- Free to travel
- Free to rest and sleep fully
- Enjoy work
- Human rights protected
- Helping out each other
- Can concentrate and learn
- Feel loved
- Not distinguished by ethnic group
- Brave
- Mutual respect
- Free to practice one's faith
- Lots of energy
- Interested in meeting others
- Free exchange of ideas
- Trust ones' self and others
- Interested in learning & knowing
- Calm
- Know one's self
- Free to change

Give each person a piece of paper and spread out crayons, pencils and other coloring materials. Tell them, *"You will be using these materials later. Right now get in a comfortable position to sit awhile, close your eyes if that's okay, and imagine a place that you feel really safe. Maybe this is a real place that you know or a place in your imagination. Begin to look around your safe place while I am talking; notice the details. I don't know where you are, that's up to you. Maybe you are outside in nature, or maybe you are inside; it's up to you. Maybe you are alone or maybe you are with friends or other people. Maybe there are no other people, or some other people or lots of other people, whatever makes you feel safe. Look around your safe place, what can you see? What colors do you see? What can you smell? What can you hear? Whenever you want to come here you can, because this place belongs to you. In a minute, or right now, you are feeling very safe. Take a moment to feel what this feels like."* Give them time, then say, *"Snap dragon"* or *"Frog"* or any word that is concrete and a bit surprising. Then say, *"Okay, it is now time to open our eyes. Take your paper and draw a picture of your safe place. There are lots of colors, you are free to use as many colors as you'd like. Remember the colors in your imagination. If you need another color, you may look for it or ask for it. Please write at the top like this."* Show an example of '_[Name]_'s Safe Place.' *"You will use this picture later in this workshop, so please keep it where you can find it later."*

After they have worked for awhile and someone is getting close to finishing, say, *"Excuse me just a moment. Please write three words on your picture, any words you would like, anywhere you would like, but pick three words to write and write them on your picture somewhere. Remember, this is your own place and you can remember this place whenever you would like during this workshop or after you go home."*

When some people are done writing, ask if everybody can finish in three to five minutes or if anyone still needs a lot more time. When group time is running out, say, *"Okay, our time is up. Please find a partner to talk to about what it felt like and what you learned from doing this activity. If you would like, you may show your picture and describe it but you do NOT have to. Please take about three to five minutes each to talk. When you're done, please come back to the large group, pick up the crayons and pencils, then sit quietly in the circle until everyone is back."*

Debriefing
Return to the large group and ask:
"Is there anything you would like to say before we move on?"

Transforming Power

Purposes
To remember transforming power and the materials we received on it in the Alternatives to Violence Project Basic workshop; to encourage referring to and practicing explicitly opening up to transforming power.

Time
25 minutes.

Materials
Transforming Power Cards and/or a Transforming Power Mandala.

Instructions
Put the mandala on the floor and give everyone a Transforming Power Card. Stay in the large group or divide the group into small groups of three to five and ask them to discuss *"What is the connection between transforming power and trauma healing?"* Give the small groups ten minutes to discuss this.

Debriefing
Ask them to come back to the large group and have each small group share one important connection they made.

Concentric Circles

Purposes
To start to break down barriers by getting people talking to each other. To get to know ourselves and others on topics of importance. To realize how much we can share in short amounts of time. To remember and talk about powerful experiences of the past in smaller segments of time and then move on to someone or something else, realizing that there is life after and outside of that past experience.

Time
Approximately six minutes for each question plus fifteen for debriefing.

Materials
Three to five questions jointly agreed upon by the team.

Instructions
Arrange people in two concentric circles, one facing in and one facing out, matching each person on the outside with someone on the inside. Have partners introduce themselves. *"You and your partner will take turns talking about a topic I will give you. When you are listening, you are ONLY listening; do not make comments or enter into discussion. Respect your partner's pauses to think. After I give you the topic, you will have a few moments of silence to think about it and then I will say, 'begin' and you will have two or three minutes to talk. The outside circle will speak first."* Read a topic. Give them 15-20 seconds of silence, then say, *"Begin."* After two to three minutes, call *"Switch."* And repeat the topic. After two or three minutes, call *"Stop. Thank your partner. Now the outside circle stand up and move one person to your right."* For the subsequent topics alternate inside and outside circles to begin speaking and rotate to the right after each question has been answered by both persons. The team selects the questions to be used based on the whole facilitation team's sense of the needs and strengths of the group.

Select from the topics below or create your own. If you create your own, try it out in the team clinic before using it with the whole group.

- Things I respect in myself are….
- A person I admire and why….

- How I see transforming power related to trauma healing is….
- A time I almost gave up on life but got support or strength to carry on….

- Ways I show respect for myself are….
- Ways I take care of myself are….

- Qualities I look for in a friend are….
- A positive influence in my life right now is….
- An important life lesson I have learned in my life is….

- A time I did the right thing even though I felt fear was….
- A part of me that I really want to change is….

- A time I felt really happy was….
- Ways other people can help me become the person I want to be is….
- One thing I want to accomplish in the next year is….

Remember to begin and end on a positive topic. The first one brings out the strengths and resources of the speaker; the last one engages those strengths and resources in the speakers life and/or future.

Debriefing
What did you notice from doing this activity?
What did it feel like to do this activity?
Did you find it difficult to talk/listen for that long without changing roles?
How did you react when there was silence?
What will you take home from doing this?

Closing: Breathing

Purposes
To get to know ways to take care of, sooth and affirm ourselves.

Time: 5 minutes.

Materials: None.

Instructions
"Remember caring for ourselves is very important in this work. Ways to take care of ourselves may be different than ways to sooth ourselves. Self care are things we do to take care of ourselves so that we have good health in the long run. Self-soothing techniques are things we do in the moment to calm or modulate emotion, anxiety or arousal. Breathing well can be both."

Invite everyone to sit up straight and close their eyes if they would like and say slowly: *"Feel your breath. Feel the breath come in and feel the breath go out, feel the breath come in and feel the breath go out. Feel the breath pass into your nose and mouth and down your throat and into your chest. Notice the air going in and notice the air going out. In. Out. In. Out. Feel your body as a channel for the air. Breath is Life. I am Alive. I am Here. As you breathe in, feel life being given to you freely and as you breathe out, feel release of all difficulties and tensions. As the air comes in you're given life; as the air goes out you may release life's difficulties and tensions."* Give a bit of quiet time before moving on.

Variation: You may add, with people sitting or lying on the floor, *"Very gently, tighten the muscles in your legs as you take a breath; hold your breath while I count to three* (seconds); *now let your muscles and breath go; and rest."* Be sure to encourage relaxation and gentleness as a preparation or some people may get cramps if they are not able to relax as well as to tense. Repeat this twice for each body part: knees to the feet, only feet, elbows to the hands, hands only, back, shoulders, arms and back, abdominal area, face, eyes, cheeks, mouth, chin. *"Sit or lie still for a moment and feel the body relax, notice your breath, the feeling of the pressure as the breath enters, the feeling of relaxation as the breath goes out. Notice how your body feels at this moment."* [Pause.] *"Notice how the body feels from head to foot."*

REMEMBERING: SESSION III

Gathering: Name and *one person who loves me is*....
Agenda Preview
Empty Chair
Grounding: One Object
Light & Lively: Sounding Circle
Loss, Grief and Mourning
Light & Lively: Turn Up the Volume
Self Care: Breathing
Stories of Trauma

Empty Chair

Purposes
To identify important personal or spiritual strengths and resources for each person.

Time: 45 minutes.

Materials: None

Instructions: *"Each person stands behind his or her chair and takes the role of a person who loves them; it may be the person you named in the gathering or someone else. Looking at the chair, as if you are still sitting there, say, 'My name is… and my relationship to [your name] is… and I love and care about him/her because….' Give the reasons that she or he loves you."* The facilitator may want to begin in order to model how the activity works.

Debriefing
After this activity, you must debrief with companions or small groups, but you may also come back to the large group and share insights:
What did you notice from doing this activity?
How did it feel to do this activity?
What did you learn from doing this activity?
How does this relate to transforming power and healing from trauma?

Grounding: One Object

Time: 3-5 minutes.

Materials: Found objects at the moment of the activity.

Instructions: *"At this moment, you are very safe. Notice all the goodwill around you. We are now going to do an activity called 'One Object.' Take a small object in your hand—whatever you can reach, a small stone, a pen, a cell phone, whatever. Look at the shape and describe it in as much detail as possible—its color, texture, size, shape, read any writing, what it is used for and so forth."*

Loss, Grief and Mourning

Purposes
To introduce loss, grief and mourning to be sure that each person has a sense of the definition of each and can distinguish between them.

Time: 40 minutes.

Materials: Three posters with titles and definitions for:
- Loss: Something or someone important that we can never meet or have again.
- Grief: A personal, emotional reaction of deep sadness or sorrow in response to a great loss of a relationship, person or thing.
- Mourning: Time set aside personally or with family and community to remember and pay our respects for who or what was lost and discharge our grief over the loss.

Instructions
In the large group, discuss the definitions of each of the three before brainstorming examples under the definitions. *"What are major losses in your life?" "What does it feel like to have a great loss?" "What are ways you grieve significant losses in your life?" "How do you discharge your grief?" "What are ways your family, religious group or community mourn losses?" "What ways help you to heal? What ways seem to keep you from healing?"* After brainstorming all three, step back and give people time to look at them. Allow any reflections to be shared. Often debriefing happens spontaneously and does not need to be prompted.

Light and Lively: Turn Up the Volume

Time: 15-20 minutes (no materials).

Instructions: Have people rotate being the "conductor" who stands in front of the group, names an emotion and then moves his or her hands on a continuum from high to low, up and down. All the others use their bodies, facial expressions and voices to express that emotion to that degree, high to low, depending on where the conductor's hands are. Switch conductors. You may debrief this Light and Lively.

VARIATION: Experiences of Grief

Purposes
To help people understand that there are many ways to experience loss, grief and mourning. To practice expressing loss, grief and mourning in a safe place as a natural experience.

Time: 30 minutes.

Materials
Small cards (15 cards x 24 participants = 360 cards with one to two words on each card). Make one stack of cards for each resulting in 15 stacks: Denial/Numbness, Avoidance, Realization, Why Me?, Anger, Bargaining, Abandonment, Guilt, Remorse, Anxiety, Physical Problems, Apathy, Hopelessness, Acceptance, Adjustment. The total number of cards in each stack is greater than or equal to the number of participants.

Instructions
Place the fifteen stacks of cards in the center of the circle. Explain that each person may experience grief in different ways at different times. *"Remember a time you experienced a loss. What did the grief feel like afterwards? How many different ways did you experience grief at different times, in different places with different people or when you were alone?"* Pause. *"One-by-one, please come forward and take a single card for each word that describes how you have experienced grief personally. As you take the card, demonstrate physically what it means to you. You may take a card from as many stacks as you like, but take only one card from each stack, not the whole stack."* Demonstrate as you speak. When they are thinking of their losses, simple physical instructions can be difficult. *"Take your cards back to your companions and take three to five minutes for each person to talk about how they experience grief."* The facilitator gives a warning at three minutes, calls switch and closes. After each person has gone, they might want to write the words from their cards in their journal, then ask them to return the cards neatly to the piles in the center one-by-one. Return to the large group for debriefing.

Debriefing
What did you notice? What does this feel like? What did you learn? What will you take home from this activity?

Stories of Trauma

Purposes
To remember traumatic experiences in a structured manner so not to relive or reenact those experiences, but to reprocess and discharge them.

Time: Approximately 120 minutes, followed by a break when finished.

Materials: One VoC handout, seven to ten writing sheets and a pen for each participant and coloring supplies: pencils, crayons, pastels, etc… spread around to be available to everyone. Example of seven sentences written out on the bottom of seven landscaped sheets taped to the wall. Two flip chart sheets taped to the wall with the following printed on them:

> **Tell about One Situation**
> - Where it occurred.
> - The concrete facts of what happened.
> - How it felt to you at that time.
> - How you knew when it was over.

> **Complete These Sentences**
> 1. I was startled when….
> 2. I felt like there was no way out when….
> 3. I froze when….
> 4. I felt like… (chose something like one of these)
>   … I had no pain or couldn't breath when….
>   … I was outside myself just watching when….
>   … I lost feeling of my body when….
> 5. I did what I was told or what I could, which was….
> 6. I knew it was over at least for now when….
> 7. In order to feel better, I ….

Instructions

Ask all participants to get their safe place picture. *"Take good care of yourself as you do this activity. You already have a number of methods—groundings, SUD Scale one to ten, breathing and so forth. If you need to rest or walk for a few minutes or go wash your face with cool water, just let your companion and a facilitator know and go do it. Please get with a partner, preferably your companion and get ten sheets of paper and a pen for each of you and coloring supplies, such as crayons, pastels or colored pencils to share for drawing. Please set these aside to use later. Choose who will speak first."* Give time to get materials and choose the first speaker. *"Now please read again 'A Good Listening Companion.'"* Again, give time to read.

"The speaker will tell a story about a traumatic or very difficult personal experience. The companion will listen. To learn a new technique, start with a moderately difficult experience not the most difficult one. I will give you a minute to think of a situation. If you have selected an incident, please tell your companion (point on the wall as you read them):

- *Where it occurred.*
- *The concrete facts of what happened.*
- *How it felt to you at that time.*
- *How you knew when it was over.*

You will have about ten minutes each to tell the story." Pause to think of a time. *"Once you thought of a time, fill out the VoC Scale then tell your story."* After eight minutes say, *"The first speaker should be finishing up now."* After ten minutes say, *"Switch."* After another ten minutes with a warning, say *"You need to finish the story now."* If anyone is taking much longer to tell a story, a facilitator may listen in for a bit and then help the person move along.

"You will support each other in completing seven sentences." Read each of the sentences from the wall. *"At first it may feel like splitting hairs, like all these things happened at the same time, but if you give yourself a little time to think, you can usually come up with different parts of the event for each sentence. See what image comes to mind for each sentence. Write each of the sentences across the bottom of a page. Remember to number them! After you've written all the sentences, draw a picture for each sentence. As you write and draw, you may remember more details about the incident. Go ahead and fill the details in. When you are done drawing, check to see if you would add cartoon bubbles for things people said or were thinking. Please work silently."* When people begin to finish up, say: *"When you are done, please see if you want to add any more*

cartoon bubbles for what people said or were thinking, then put the safe place picture on the top with the other seven piled behind it. Everyone may take a break when done drawing, but please make it a quiet break in respect for those still working."

After the break, gather in the large group all persons with their eight sheets of paper. Assign each pair to a separate space. Large rooms can have two or three pairs on separate walls if they are not too close to one another, but each pair needs its own space.

Ask each pair to trade papers, so they are holding the other person's papers. *"When you are in your place, decide whose story is taped up first—he or she sits in a chair facing the wall. The partner will tape the pictures on the wall like this."* Show the two rows of four landscaped pages as the example on the wall. While demonstrating with a volunteer in a chair facing the wall, say *"The person in the chair looks over the story and, when ready, says, "Okay, I'm ready." Then, very slowly, the person standing points to the Safe Place and reads <u>exactly</u> what is on the paper with pauses between each text. NOT more; NOT less; just what was written on the paper. Continue to read each sentence first, then any cartoon bubbles on the sheet, pausing between each sheet, until you have read everything there. It is disrespectful and ineffective to add, skip, make jokes, laugh or comment at this time. If you feel the urge to add an introduction or closing or any other words, <u>resist!</u> After you finish reading the papers, step back and be silent. Give the person time to look at the story on the wall. When the person seated is ready, say, 'Okay, I'm done.' After that take the pictures down and give them back to the person seated. Trade positions and repeat this process."*

Return to the large group, ask them all to get their VoC sheet out and fill in the second table, notice any changes and save it with their Safe Place and Story. These papers are their own. Tell them to put them in a safe place right now before the debriefing, closing or break.

Debriefing
What did you notice from doing this activity?
What did it feel like to do this? What did you learn from doing this?
How do you experience transforming power and healing in this?

MOURNING: SESSION IV

Gathering: Name and *two words for how I feel right now are*....
Agenda Preview
Positive Moments Sculpture
Companions: A Good Companion
Self Care: Massage
Light & Lively: Wake Up in the Forest
River of Life
Grounding: Fingers
Evaluation of the Day
Closing

Positive Moments Sculpture

Purposes
To find ways to honor and grieve losses. To remember good aspects of significant losses.

Time
Depends on the time left and needs of the group (they may be tired).

Materials
None.

Instructions
"At difficult times, there is often no time or opportunity to honor the losses. This activity gives time to remember the positive and meaningful moments of traumatic incidents or of the relationship, person or thing that was lost." Ask everyone to tape their pictures on the wall or look at them and remember some aspect of that moment or loss that was positive and meaningful. One-by-one, stand in front of your pictures or step forward into the group and briefly name a positive and meaningful aspect from that time. Tell everyone, *"Please pick people from the large group or get props from around the room to make a sculpture of that meaningful moment or aspect. Tell people where and how to stand, what they are feeling, what they are doing, what facial expression to have. If you would like them to make a movement or say a phrase or sentence you may show or tell them what to do."* Once the sculpture is made, stand back to look at it. Ask the sculptor, *"Does the sculpture represents the positive aspect that you wanted to show? If you want to change it, please feel free to do that now."* Then step back again and look at it. Ask, *"Is there something you will take home from this memory?"* After everyone has had a chance to make a sculpture, give them all time to remember the positive aspect of that moment that they sculpted. Not everyone has to do it.

Debriefing
Return to the large group and ask the group to be silent, sing or pray. Remind them that it is a good activity to write about afterwards in their journals.

River of Life

Purposes
To think about traumatic experiences in the context of our whole lives. To integrate traumatic experiences into the longer narrative of our lives.

Time
One hour.

Materials
A large piece of drawing paper, markers, crayons and colored pencils for each person.

Instructions
Give everyone a large piece of paper, markers, crayons and colored pencils. *"Please think about your life as a river and draw along the river the events that have shaped who you are. The source of the river is your birth. It flows to the present and on into the future. Add important people or places if you want. You may draw a road, path or other thing that represents your life if you want. You may write words on the drawing. If you don't want to draw, you may write. You each work silently by yourself. You will be sharing your picture in a small group when you are done. You do have the right to pass, if you do not want to share."*

When people begin to finish, ask how much more time they need. Give them up to five or ten minutes more. Ask those who are finished to take a break, but be quiet in respect to those still working. When everyone is done, return to the large group. Form groups of four. Ask for three volunteers to join you in demonstrating. The facilitator places his or her picture on the floor in the center of the circle. The other three group members sit and place their pictures on the floor to their right. The facilitator stands up and steps to the side of the paper and says, *"This is the place that represents the past."* Step to the bottom, *"This is the place that represents the present."* Step to the other side, *"And this is the place that represents the future."* Explain to people as you act it out, *"Ask one person from the small group to help and another to record in writing what is said. The person whose picture is on the floor stands by the present and the helper stands by the past representing this person in the past. The person says to the helper all the strengths and gifts that have helped her survive and get where she is today. Then they switch places and the helper repeats as closely to the speaker's words as possible all the strengths and gifts that have brought her there. The recorder may give the helper notes to read. Then the helper stays in the present and the person moves to the future. The future self says to the helper representing the present self all the strengths and gifts that have helped her survive and get where she is in the future. The helper listens closely and the recorder writes. Then the person switches with the helper and the helper repeats what he has heard to the person, using the recorder's notes, while the person stands in the present place. Then give the person the notes. The person may make any final comments before sitting down. Each person in the group takes a turn placing his or her picture in the center, repeating these steps."*

VARIATION ON THIS ACTIVITY

A facilitator asks someone to talk about his drawing in the large group. Three chairs are set up labeled: past, present and future. The person explains his picture briefly while changing seats from the perspective of the past to the present to the future seat. As he moves to a new seat, the facilitator asks him: *"What were/are some the strengths and resources that helped/will help you?"* Another group member records his responses. The person stands up and the facilitator helps him make a short sculpture of a future scene using other participants as needed. From his future, he tells his present self what he needs to do to help himself reach his goal(s). Then he sits back in the present and makes sure he understood the ideas of what he needs to do to work towards the future he wants. Finally, he may make a last comment to the past and to the future and then from his place in the present.

Return to the large group after everyone is given a chance to explain their drawing from the seats.

Debriefing
What did you notice from doing this?
What did it feel like to do this activity?
What new learning did you get from doing this?
What will you take home and do differently because of this?
How is this related to transforming power, healing from trauma and living nonviolently?

RECONNECTING: SESSION V

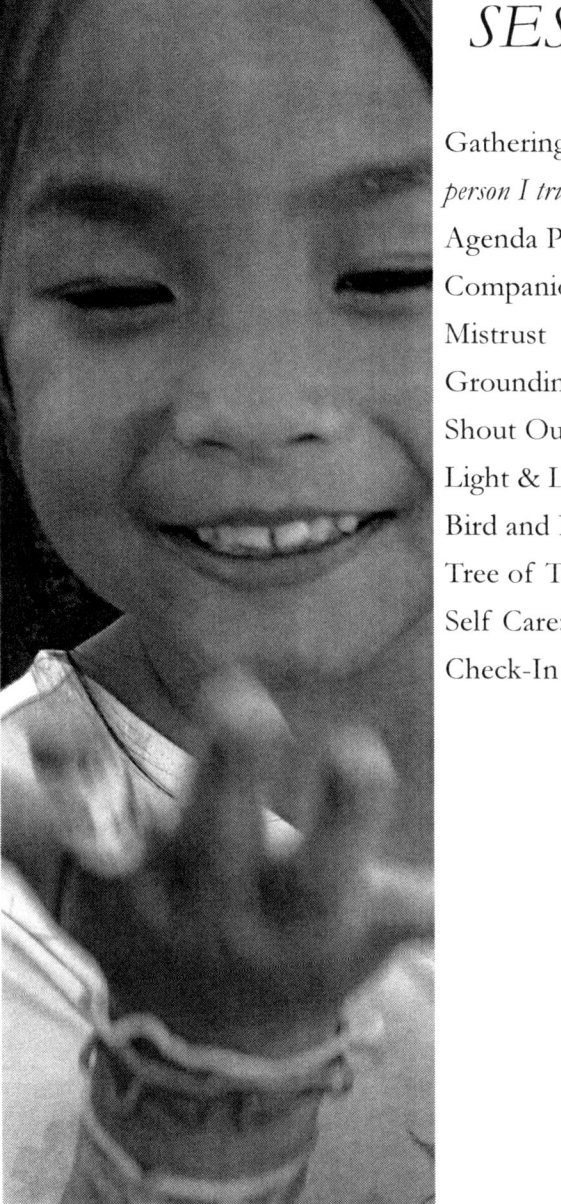

Gathering: Name and *one person I trust and why*....

Agenda Preview

Companions: Trust and Mistrust

Grounding: 3, 2, 1

Shout Out

Light & Lively: Elephant, Bird and Palm Tree

Tree of Trust

Self Care: Self Soothing

Check-In

Speak Out

Purposes
To recognize secondary trauma and break the silence.

Time: 60 minutes.

Material: Poster paper and markers for each group of three. Three sheets titled:
"Times We're Witnesses/Bystanders to Violence"
"How it Feels to be Witnesses/Bystanders to Violence"
"Ways to Respond as Witnesses/Bystanders to Violence"
Also post on the wall:

> ### Secondary Trauma
> Symptoms of trauma experienced after you:
> - Witness violence
> - Treat victims of violence
> - Hear stories of violence
>
> Share about violence you witnessed or heard:
> - I am speaking to....
> - What I saw or heard was....
> - How it was wrong is....
> - It broke my heart/made me mad because....
> - What has to change is....

Instructions
"The best way to alleviate secondary trauma is to <u>reprocess the primary traumas</u> of one's life. Once one has attended to these, there is still work that can be done to clear symptoms from secondary trauma. Crimes and injustices don't just happen to the people directly involved, they also decrease safety for everyone in the community. <u>To publicly declare an injustice happened</u>, that it was wrong and should not have happened is critical for restoring safe, healthy lives for victims, perpetrators and the community. <u>To seek and take actions</u> to prevent other crimes or injustices from happening in the future is a significant second step."

"Violence traumatizes victims, but also the people who witness the violence, treat the victims, or hear the stories and news afterwards; this is called secondary trauma (Gentry). Secondary trauma produces the same effects as primary trauma to varying degrees in varying manners, but the symptoms are the same."

Brainstorm for about ten minutes on:
- Times We're Witnesses or Bystanders to Violence
- How it Feels to be Witnesses or Bystanders to Violence
- Ways to Respond as Witnesses or Bystanders to Violence

Make groups of three. *"Think of violence or injustice you've witnessed or heard about that breaks your heart or makes you mad; remember to stay at a five or less on the SUD Scale and do a grounding if you need to reduce your distress. Think of how you felt and what you would like to say about it to whom.* Point to the poster as you speak. *"I'll give you three to five minutes per person to speak to these five items.*
- *I am speaking to… (a specific person, an institution, a policy maker, the public, the people in front of you, whomever you want).*
- *What I saw or heard was….*
- *How it was wrong is….*
- *It broke my heart/made me mad because….*
- *What has to change is….*

After that, <u>all together</u> for one minute, shout, talk, cry, whatever you need, but you must Speak Out about the injustice you just described for the whole minute. If you come to the end of what you had to express, start again at the beginning and repeat it over and over. Don't get quiet. Don't stop. The facilitator will remind you to keep going, don't be quiet, ask, "What has to change?" After you shout out, write whatever statements are important to post for the 'public' with markers on these posters. Each group should have a poster and markers."

Debrief
Return to the large group. Share each group's poster and invite feelings and insights. Post the posters on a wall together. Do a grounding technique as a group to come back to present time.

Note: "Companions: Discharge" on what it's like to be a helpless witness or silent bystander is a good follow-up activity if there is time.

Tree of Trust

Purposes
To identify causes and results of trust and to look in more detail at the strengths and supports that are needed to build a trusting community.

Time
40 minutes.

Materials
1-2 leaves, a fruit (e.g. mango or apple) and a root for each participant and a trunk and branches.

Instructions
"We cannot reach our hopes and goals by ourselves. Our hopes are a part of our community and environment. What environment do we need to support our hopes for the future? In that environment, what are the roots that are not seen by others, but we know must be there to make this future possible? What do people do that is not seen that make this community possible? And what are the results, the leaves and fruits, of those roots that we do see? What do you see around in a trusting community?" Pass out 1-2 leaves and one fruit (mango/apple) and one root to each person and ask them to write as much as they want on each one. After they write, ask them to come up one at a time to the trunk of the tree, slowly and clearly read each of their roots and tape them to the tree. Repeat this for the leaves and fruits together. It helps to have a facilitator putting the tape on the upper side, not the stem, of the leaf or mango/apple, but let the participants tape them on the tree. After everyone has taped their roots, leaves and fruit to the tree, have some quiet time to gaze at the tree.

Debriefing
What do you see here?
What steps do you need to take in your life to get the results you want?
How has this exercise helped you better sense transforming power in your life?

WRAPPING UP: SESSION VI

Gathering: Name and *one thing I'll take home with me is*....
Agenda Preview
Whisper Circle
Tracking and Balancing
Grounding: Pleasant Memories
Open Questions
Next Steps
Evaluation
Closing: Goodbye Circle

Whisper Circle

Purposes
To contradict negative messages embedded as internal recordings from past experience and to give people an experience of deep affirmation.

Time
40 minutes.

Materials
One 3 x 5 note card for each person and a pen for each person.

Instructions
Pass out a note card and pen to each person. Tell people to: *"Remember a negative message about yourself from when you were small or one that's stuck with you. Write it on the card briefly, clearly and legibly without your name. On the opposite side of the card write briefly, clearly and legibly the contradiction or antidote for that message."* Collect all the cards. Ask half of the people to sit in a circle facing in and the other half to stand behind someone in a chair. Shuffle the cards with the positive messages up. Give the standing people each two cards with the positive messages up. Ask them to make sure they do not have their own card. If someone does, just exchange it across the circle. Ask them to make sure they can read both cards before starting. Ask if people prefer the lights off or down. Keep the space calm. Demonstrate how to read; whisper the first message in the LEFT ear, whisper the second message in the RIGHT ear, then move to the LEFT ear of the next person. Begin, everyone whispering a message into another person's LEFT ear, then another message into the RIGHT ear, repeating that for every person in the circle. When you're done, pause a moment and let people in the circle feel what that was like. Then switch the groups. Pause again to let that group feel what it was like. Then slowly return to the large group.

Debriefing
What did you notice from doing this activity?
What did that feel like?
What did you learn from that exercise?
What does this exercise tell you about transforming power and healing?

Tracking and Balancing

Purposes
To learn to monitor, balance and take care of one's own emotional life. To have a tool that works well when one is not at one's best, good for adults and for teenagers or young adults, especially when they move away from home.

Time
20 minutes.

Materials
"Tracking How I Feel" and "Balancing How I Feel" handout for each participant. Each sheet may be copied two to a side and front to back, then cut or folded in two horizontally and stapled together to make a small booklet. You may make booklets as part of what you give each participant for coming to the workshop, or you may just give them a copy of the sheet, but it is nice to copy two of each side-by-side so if someone wants to make a booklet, it is easy to do with the sheets they are given.

Instructions
Hand out both sheets to everyone, then say: *"Notice that at the top of the sheet one reads 'TRACKING How I Feel' and one reads 'BALANCING How I Feel.' Please look at Tracking first. On the left side, there is a scale from positive five to negative five. Each person must write his or her own descriptors on this scale. There are no right or wrong answers. Some people write their scale in terms of energy, mood or other factors, but each person is different both in the scale and in the "normal" or "desirable" pattern over time. When you have written in your scale on the left side, you may either put a date above each X across the top OR you may write the date with times of day, using several X's for one day. The latter allows you to track your energy or mood swings across the day, the former across the weeks or months. But which you use depends on what you feel the need to track. Each day you make a mark along the vertical X's that describes your feeling and draw a line from one mark to the next creating a graph. This is a powerful tool for seeing your natural rhythm of energy and mood cycles or swings and tracking your sense of health. Remember extreme highs can be as detrimental as extreme lows. If you feel you are struggling, look at the balancing activities at the bottom. Pick a few (1-3 is best, but no more than 5) that you think will make the most positive difference*

for yourself and circle them at the top of the 'BALANCING7 How I Feel' sheet, again write the dates and/or dates with times across the top for each X, and then decide how you will track each of these items. Sharing this with your listening companion is a terrific personal accountability method. Right now, fill in your scale, mark where you remember yourself being in the last two days and today and consider if there is an action plan of three to five things you would like to do for yourself. If there are, circle them at the top of 'BALANCING How I Feel' sheet or write in others that do not appear there and fill in as much as you remember about those things over the past two days and today."

Debriefing

"When both people are done, share with your partner what it felt like to do this. You may or may not wish to share the contents of your sheets; you do not have to if you do not wish to. Take three to five minutes each to share. When you are done, come back to the large group to share any compelling feelings or insights."

Appendices

Appendix I: Companion Sessions

Purposes
To practice listening with interest and relaxed concern. To practice talking more deeply about personally difficult experiences and discharging the emotions associated with them. To practice ways of accompanying each other in the work of healing.

Time: 20 minutes each meeting.

Materials: Typically none.

Instructions
"Find a partner who lives near you and may be able to meet again after this workshop if you choose to do so. For now, however, the only commitment is to support each other through the course of this workshop. Look over the posters: "Physical Discharge of Emotional Stress" and "A Good Listening Companion." Remember, this is what we are practicing. Be sure both people get equal time—so you must keep track of time. Give half the minutes to the first person, switch at the given time and give the other half to the second person, even if one or both are quiet for some time, be patient and wait to see if more is expressed." Examples of variations for these sessions are below.

Debrief for Various Companions Sessions
What did you notice? What did it feel like to do this activity?
What did you like or not like about listening?
What did you like or not like about speaking?
What did you learn from this activity?
How is this related to healing and nonviolence?
What will you take home from this activity?

Ways I Receive Help…
"Decide who goes first. Say your name and talk about: 'Things people do that make me feel helped and supported are….' Take turns being the speaker and the listener and speak for three to five minutes. I will say when to switch. After both persons have spoken, you will be given a few minutes (3-5minutes) just to talk together about giving and receiving help."

Journal

Introduce the idea of a journal (see Appendix III: Self Care, page 74), then invite companions to write two to three points that are important for them, that they have learned, or that they will take home with them. If they don't like to write, they may draw or reflect on the question silently, after which they can share in pairs on the topic.

Debriefing on Guides for Companions

After each person is sitting in a pair, say: *"Look back at the materials on being a good companion and choose who will speak first. Each person takes three minutes to talk about his or her strengths and weaknesses as a companion. Be sure your partner starts with specific strengths before naming weaknesses. I'll tell you when to switch. After that I'll give you five minutes to discuss being a good listening companion in your pair."* Other topics include: experiences of trust and mistrust; on being a good companion; ways I grieve and ways I might try grieving in the future; how transforming power is related to healing from trauma and rebuilding social relationships; or any other topic.

Discharge

After each person is sitting in a pair, say, *"Please look back at the 'Physical Discharge of Emotional Stress.' Choose who will speak first and who will be the companion. Remember that the companion is to listen with interest and relaxed concern to permit and encourage discharge, without being carried away with emotion. The speaker will take five minutes to remember a problem or painful event and notice how the body responds. Recall one of the scariest, saddest or most enraging times in your life and try to enter into feeling it rather than just retelling it. What do you feel in your body? … and where? What specific physical discharge do you feel welling up? Don't inhibit the physical response; allow it to occur. You may speak, but you do not have to. It may help to make noises that arise. Allow the discharge while you remember the event or problem. When it is time to switch roles, use a grounding technique or two to "bring yourself back" before becoming a listening companion to the other person. Realize that this is not easy; it is an opportunity to notice any feelings of physical discharge in your body."* Follow this with a Light and Lively or group grounding technique to make certain that everyone comes back from this experience.

Appendix II: Grounding Techniques

Purposes
To give short, simple, effective techniques to use when distress levels rise to the point that a person begins to get carried away with emotion, in other words when the person begins to "daydream," "fly," lose language or dissociate. To help a person come back to their senses and be grounded in the present. To increase a person's capabilities to bring themselves back to present time using techniques that are easy to use in any setting.

Time
3-5 minutes.

Materials
None needed for most of these, except any object laying around for "An Object" and a gong for "Gong."

Instructions
We introduce a grounding after activities that are likely to trigger distress in people. Begin by saying, *"Now is a good time to do a grounding, since you just paid attention to something that may have been distressful. We use groundings when we are distressed by memories of past difficulties to help us return to present time. At this moment, you are very safe. Notice all the goodwill around you. We are now going to do…."* Repetition of the same words every time at the opening creates a "voice" that may come to them when they need it. Keep them simple, without extra talking. Examples of groundings are:

In This Chair (or On This Floor)
While sitting in a circle, say to everyone, *"Feel your bottom on your chair (or floor). Notice the legs of the chair go down to the floor. Notice the floor goes out to the walls and the walls go into the foundation of the building. Notice the foundation goes into the ground and the ground spreads out to be the town of* [Name] *which is on the earth and the earth is a large ball of mass in the universe. The universe supports the earth, which supports the town of* [Name]*, which supports this plot of ground, which supports the foundation of this building, which supports the walls, which supports the floor, which supports the chair, which supports me. I am supported by all of this."*

An Object
"Take a small object in your hand—whatever you can reach, a small stone, a pen, a cell phone, whatever. Look at the object and describe it in as much detail as possible—its color, texture, size, shape, read any writing on it, what it is used for and so forth."

3 2 1
"Look around above eye level and name three thing you can see, three things you can touch, three things you can hear; now two thing you can see, two things you can touch, two things you can hear; then one thing you can see, one thing you can touch, and one thing you can hear."

Fingers
Ask everyone to raise two fingers (index and middle finger on one hand) in front of their face and have their eyes follow the two fingers as they move from one side of the body to the other, crossing the center line of the body, weaving through the air. Stop a moment, rest and repeat.

Closed Eyes
Remind people that emotion builds inside. If the emotion is too high, then this approach may make it worse, not better. So, use this activity when it helps. If it makes you feel worse, stop immediately and use "An Object" or "3, 2, 1." When you are ready, close your eyes and remember your personal safe place, then ask yourself what it is you need right now. Before opening your eyes, say a concrete but unusual word such as "Snapdragon," "Frog" or "What color is my shirt?" Something that pulls you into present time.

Silence
Invite the group to sit silently. Ten minutes is good; twenty will take people deeper. When you feel the group has become calm and centered and it is time to move on, simply say, *"Thank you."* You may take hands on either side around the circle or shake the persons' hands beside you.

Five-Letter Word
Suggest a five-letter word. Ask people to think of geographic places, types of food, or other categories, that begin with each of the five letters.

Pleasant Memories

Ask everyone to sit comfortably. *"I will talk you through a few steps to recall a pleasant memory. When we get to the step where you are actually feeling really good and happy, we want to imprint that memory with a physical code. You may pick your own physical code, but often it is gently pinching or rubbing the skin between your thumb and first finger with the opposite hand. Whichever hand you use, always use the same hand when imprinting or recalling pleasant memories. So right now gently pinch or rub the skin between your thumb and first finger or pick your own simple, tactile action."* [Pause.] *"Okay, now stop."* [Pause.] *"Now, relax your breathing. Relax your eyes. Relax your mind. Smile. Remember a pleasant memory. Try to use all your senses to remember this pleasant memory fully. What colors do you see? What and who are around you? What sounds do you hear? What is the air like? As you feel the full goodness or happiness of the memory, do the action you have chosen."* Give the participants time to recall and rub their hand. When you see everyone doing their action for a bit, then say, *"Okay, you can come back now. If you do this frequently, whenever you need to shift your mood or energy, you can repeat your action while recalling pleasant thoughts and the memories and feelings will tend to come to you more quickly even in difficult times and circumstances."*

Gong

If you have a gong, you may use it. Say to everyone, *"If it's comfortable to do so, close your eyes; if not, that's okay, but if your eyes get heavy you may close them later. Let your mind follow the sound."* Hit the gong and wait until the sound is completely gone.

Walk or Run

If someone is carried away with emotion, invite them to a safe, quiet place away from others. Give them a moment to adjust to being out of the group. If they still don't feel they can rejoin the group, invite them to go outside with you and walk really fast. If that doesn't work, then run. After a bit you can return. If someone "goes berserk," then take them outside to walk or run.

Appendix III: Self Care and Soothing

Purposes
To get to know specific options for self-care activities that help maintain and protect long-term health. To get to know specific options for self-soothing activities that help calm or modulate emotion, anxiety or arousal in the moment. To practice concrete ways to respect and affirm one's self.

Time: 5-20 minutes.

Materials: Journal or sports equipment.

Instructions
When you first do self care with the group during "Stand on a Line" or smaller activity, briefly make the distinction: *"Self care is activities to maintain and protect long-term health and self soothing is activities to calm or modulate emotion, anxiety or arousal in the moment. To respect and affirm ourselves, we need to practice doing both."* Examples of variations for these activities are below.

Debriefing for Various Activities in Self Care and Self Soothing
What did you notice from doing this activity?
How did this feel like? What did you discover that was new in this?
How is this related to transforming power and healing?
What about this will you take home and do differently now?

Imagine Safety
Invite everyone to sit up and close their eyes if they want to. Slowly say: *"Feel your eyes are relaxed, your face is relaxed, you chin is relaxed, your neck is relaxed, your chest is relaxed, your whole body is relaxed. Notice your breathing. Now imagine you are in a safe place. If you don't know a safe place, just imagine if you were safe what it would feel like. What color would it be? Let that color wash over and fill you; imagine the feeling of the color inside you. What does it smell like? Remember what that smell reminds you of. Now you can touch and feel it, what does it feel like? You can see it. What do you see? This is called safety. Whenever you want you can come back here."* When they're finished, say a word or statement that is concrete and unusual or ask a random question. Then ask them to open their eyes.

Breathing

Invite everyone to sit up straight and close their eyes if they would like. Then say slowly: *"Feel your breath. Feel the breath come in and feel the breath go out, feel the breath come in and feel the breath go out. Feel the breath pass into your nose and mouth and down your throat and into your chest. Notice the air going in and notice the air going out. In. Out. In. Out. Feel your body as a channel for the air. Breath is Life. I am Alive. I am Here. As you breathe in, feel life being given to you freely and as you breathe out, feel release of all difficulties and tensions. As the air comes in you're given life; as the air goes out you may release life's difficulties and tensions."* Give a bit of quiet time before moving on.

Breathing: Variation

You may add, with people sitting or lying on the floor, *"Very gently, tighten the muscles in your legs as you take a breath; hold your breath while I count to three (seconds); now let your muscles and breath go; and rest."* Be sure to encourage relaxation and gentleness as a preparation or some people may get cramps if they are not able to relax as well as to tense. Repeat this twice for each body part: knees to the feet, only feet, elbows to the hands, hands only, back, shoulders, arms and back, abdominal area, face, eyes, cheeks, mouth, chin. *"Sit or lie still for a moment and feel the body relax, notice your breath, the feeling of the pressure as the breath enters, the feeling of relaxation as the breath goes out. Notice how your body feels at this moment."* [Pause.] *"Notice how the body feels from head to foot."*

Massage

Invite everyone to sit up straight. Say slowly: *"Let's begin to massage around the eyes, along the upper eye bone, over to the temple, out and down to the very far end of the jaw joint just below the ear, open and close your jaw gently, just a little bit so your finger can feel the very back of the jaw joint moving. Return to the bridge of the nose and come down along the cheek bone under the eye. Place two fingers between the eyebrows and go up the forehead across the top of the head to the back of the head and down to the back of the neck. Pinch the back of the neck and shoulders."* The eyes, jaw and neck have many autonomic muscles. The autonomic system is one of the oldest parts of the body. Relaxing the eyes, jaw and neck will affect our breathing, whole body, mood and energy.

Self Soothing
Brainstorm ways to calm or sooth one's self, such as prayer, bathing, going for a walk, sleeping, breathing, listening to music, playing sports, drinking tea, talking to a friend or saying positive things to one's self. Brainstorm things we do when we are anxious that make us less calm, such as smoking, drinking alcohol, going out all night, watching movies, getting busy or playing aggressively. Brainstorm, in individual journals, personal warning signs for: 1) When do I need to self sooth? 2) What are techniques or activities I find most soothing? and 3) What personal strategies would help me do these techniques when I need them?

Journal
Many approaches may be used to write in a journal. You may write or draw. Commit time to writing or just write when you need to. Ideas for journal writing include:
- Write freely.
- Write a letter to someone.
- Write a dialog between conflicting parts within yourself.
- Write a dialog between yourself and another person.
- Write a time line of hopes for the future.
- Write a time line of meaningful life moments from the past.
- Write a letter to God, a wise person or a grandparent.
- Write about an event that you would like to tell someone about.
- Write a reflection about this workshop.
- Write a reflection on a passage from a book or religious text.
- Draw a picture.
- Draw a "safety mandala."

Sports
If there are the facilities for sports, it is very good to do sports on the break. Sports are great for self care or for grounding in present time and may be physically soothing as well.

Appendix IV: Questions and Answers

The following questions have been asked at workshops. Some answers may enable facilitators to respond more clearly to participant questions; some answers may allow facilitators to understand issues better so they do not speak from misconceptions. This is a directed, experiential workshop, not a time to lecture, so often it is best to refer participants to the open questions sheet on the wall or to resources and readings rather than attempt to give answers or expert responses.

How does AVP Trauma Healing fit with traditional psychotherapy?

The Alternatives to Violence Project Advanced Trauma Healing Workshop is a group learning environment, not a one-on-one therapeutic environment. The activities in this advanced workshop are healing when done in the workshop and practiced following the workshop. The primary focus of the workshop, however, is to learn and practice language and techniques, so that participants can come to a new level of understanding and appreciation for the work of healing from trauma and can begin to use some of the language and techniques on their own following the workshop.

The facilitators commit to helping participants learn language and techniques, not to healing the participants. If a participant needs additional attention, facilitators may make effective referrals for additional counseling or therapy to be scheduled at another time, provided by someone equipped to address that individual's complexities.

In order to learn, distress must be kept to a minimum. If one has difficulty managing distress or functioning, then one needs to get in contact with a counselor or therapist. Alternatives to Violence Project facilitators should not try to fill this role or need. The AVP Advanced Trauma Healing workshop is not designed to replace one-on-one counseling or therapy.

Can one be too sympathetic when listening to someone?

Sympathy or "<u>feeling</u> with" another is a matter of emotion. Empathy or being <u>aware</u> of another's thoughts and feelings is a matter of cognition. Empathy is learned. We can increase empathy by imagining what it is like to be in another's situation and by checking our perception with that person and accepting their feedback. Sympathy expresses love and caring and supports empathy, yet being overly sympathetic leads to becoming enmeshed in the other's emotions. The critical element of listening is to listen from the heart with interest, caring and relaxed concern. As a listener, being "too sympathetic" tends to obstruct listening and healing in a number of ways:

- The speaker may not want to subject another to their pain and therefore may withhold, damper or stop their recounting.
- The listener may "steal" the speaker's experience, lose respect for the speaker's ability to handle the situation, and start "one upping" the speaker in the sense of feeling the other's emotions as much or more than the speaker.
- Rather than having a safe place to share his or her story, the speaker may feel a need to stop and "take care of" the listener.
- The listener may lose the ability to be present and provide the safety of the present that allows healing for the other person; when either listener or speaker simply relive a painful experience, they are likely to come out feeling worse.
- Too much emotional content may over-power the listener's ability to stay calmly aware of the speaker's story.

Warm, confident, unworried attention, with a focus on the speaker's goodness rather than on the details of the story, is the most useful attitude for a listening companion and will support the most healing in the other.

Compassion is vigorous empathy that gives rise to an active desire to alleviate the other's suffering. This may, however, drive us to take over, try to figure it out, fix it and rescue others from themselves, which is disrespectful and disempowering within a listening session. Simple, quiet compassion, however, may create a bond that encourages healthy friendship and mutual action in the long term.

How can I learn more about Listening Companions?

Harvey Jackins's great insights into peer co-counseling and the achievements of Re-evaluation Counseling communities have produced many insights. One of these insights is guidance for constructive ways to be present with one another while remembering and healing from trauma. People are born with great flexibility, love, curiosity, intelligence, cooperation and zest. From birth, people naturally discharge emotional and physical pain, and do so reliably if someone pays warm attention.

Counter to cultural belief, physical discharge is not a sign of hurting; it's a sign of healing. Because of this misconception, our culture teaches us to inhibit discharge until suppressing it becomes habitual. When hurts are unprocessed, they lodge inside us as blockage. We can't think flexibly when those hurts are triggered. We avoid similar circumstances or experiences. Our approach to life becomes more and more rigid and limited.

There is a spontaneous and natural way to free ourselves from the distress of past experiences, and there are reliable indicators of when this process is taking place as shown in the chart "Physical Discharge of Emotional Stress." Discharge and re-emergence from past distress follows a general sequence: grief, fear, anger, disinterest and letting go. Because of inhibitors, often the place to start is simply with engaged, non-repetitive talking. As one practices, one comes to value physical discharge and even silence as much as speaking and more easily and naturally does what one needs to support one's own healing.

Physical injury often has elements of emotional distress. With fresh physical injury, it helps to pay attention to the physical pain. With old physical injury, it's better to pay attention to the emotional content and not the memory of the physical pain. The latter may restimulate the pain.

It is recommended that facilitators practice discharging emotion to understand the perspective of these activities, but do not try to explain it if they are not trained; the activities will stand on their own. Enrolling in Re-evaluation Counseling training may enhance skills and improve the ability to respond to inquiries. Re-evaluation Counseling training is not to be mixed with other practices, however. It stands on its own.

What skills and practices help me to be a better companion listening to family members who are triggering my own stuff due to our common experiences?

Helpful skills when feeling triggered:

- Get curious and feel fluid (non-rigid); find your non-anxious presence and non-judgmental composure; think of yourself as a lighting rod, grounding their feelings rather than absorbing them; think of yourself as pipes for the other person's feelings to flow through, then imagine Love or the Living Spirit flowing through the pipes as well, keeping the pipes inside you clear and free flowing.

- Notice the place in yourself that is rigid, closed, scared or angry; take time with yourself to explore the first time you remember feeling that feeling; write, draw, retell and reflect on a narrative of that time; then approach the family member again about current concerns. As past fear and anger decline, our present tolerant, non-anxious attention increases.

- Recite a mantra of things you know are good and true about yourself. Love yourself and do your own healing so you aren't projecting your shadow onto others and trying to "fix it" in them, which will not work. Heal and love yourself well before trying to help others.

- Think before reacting. Respond instead of reacting. Change "stimulus – react" to "stimulus – observe – respond." Go into scientific mode with alert awareness, curiosity and wonder.

- Increase self-initiation, be clear with yourself about what your desired or intended result is and seek ways to get there; look for ways to enact triumph rather than re-enact trauma.

- Think of the other person as being an upset child, a vulnerable two-year-old or other age, and consider responses that encorporate tenderness into any response.

What does it mean to "lend your executive function" to assist the healing process?

Fight or flight is activated or re-activated in the right hemisphere and limbic system, or "emotional seat" of the brain, to organize for defense of self or other. An emotional overload in the limbic system shuts the gateway to the cerebral cortex where human thought occurs and reroutes it to the brain stem, reserving resources for impulsive fight or flight. When defense fails—one can neither get away nor defend oneself—one freezes, moving completely into the brain stem or reptilian brain which is autonomically reactive. When a person has the "deer in the headlights" look, he or she has retreated into the brain stem, and has no access to the cerebral cortex where human thought and executive decision-making occurs. Someone in this state cannot be expected to be "rational," but is highly suggestive. Often they will automatically follow commands or action statements.

Another person may "lend executive function," in other words help a person make decisions by "telling them what to do" until they are able to regain access to their own executive decision-making. This is true during a traumatic event or when memory of that event is triggered and the person seems to "fly away."

In this state, the propensity to be highly susceptible to suggestion is another way in which we are traumatized. As a victim, some people will find themselves "doing what they are told," which may feel like participating in the traumatizing act or they may perpetrate additional violations on others. In this manner, the perpetrator may get the victim to collude in the act or acts, leading to guilt rather than outrage and thereby protecting the actual perpetrator from natural consequences.

Ethically, one should use the practice of "lending your executive function" minimally and with great care—giving the other person just enough direction to re-establish one's access to the cortex and ability to make decisions on one's own.

Do perpetrators have traumatic reactions to what they have done?

Absolutely. Much "perpetration" is traumatic re-enactment. Perpetration can and often does re-traumatize the person and deepen self-loathing. Trauma may be re-enacted in various roles of victim, perpetrator or rescuer, enabler, bystander or silent observer. A friend from Colombia said one of the shocking effects of the violence in Colombia was that common people would hear gun shots and go to the hospital with a "morbid curiosity" to see how the people were killed. He said it was not out of compassion; it was out of needing to see it—to be a silent observer. But whether or not the incident begins a new thread of trauma or reenacts an old one, the incident may very well traumatize the perpetrator and the victim as well as any helpless witnesses who may see or hear the incident. For children, it is often worse to be in another room hearing violence against a loved one than actually seeing it occur. A friend in Aceh recounted how she grew up in a house across from a military post and as a child frequently listened to people being tortured. Hearing and seeing both may be traumatizing.

How can someone shift the balance between risks and resilience?

To shift the balance from risk to resilience in the present, one must acknowledge and resolve one's own experiences of trauma and compassion fatigue from the past. Compassion fatigue or secondary trauma are traumatic reactions we display after listening to or caring for others who experienced or are healing from trauma. We must diligently acknowledge to ourselves that avoidance and denial are part of the body's brilliance in partitioning off bad memories. What experiences have taught me about grief, fear, anger, pain or injustice? Have I processed those experiences? Do I use the tools in this workshop for myself?

Next, one must reduce known external and internal risk factors or threats to health. For most of us, making common daily decisions in our best interest may be a constant struggle. Seeking enough but not too much rest, food, sleep, work, medical care, etc., paying attention and caring for one's self, regularly engaging in soothing activities, drinking clean water and eating healthy food, and so forth. This includes saying yes to what one needs to say yes to and saying no to what one needs to say no to. It may be hard, but one needs to give up addictions to substances and to violent, deceptive or destructive relationships. Be honest and realistic with one's self about the true nature of one's relationships and the fact that one does not have control over other people's decisions. Take responsibility for one's own decisions and stay away from toxic situations, especially when one is feeling weak. Honestly attending to the simple, present things in life shifts the balance significantly from risks to resilience.

If one is doing the right things daily, then realistically talk to and affirm one's self about how well one is doing. Self-talk may replace old distressful recordings. Reducing the negative language one uses and hears and increasing the amount one smiles, laughs and feels joy significantly shifts the balance as well.

Notice, identify, expand and nurture old and new resiliency resources and skills in one's self, family, extended family, community and society, which is the rich detail and diversity of each of our lives.

Handouts

Subjective Units of Distress (SUD) Scale

A tool to communicate about how much distress
one experiences at any given moment
from zero (none) to ten (maximum).

Zero: **Asleep**–completely relaxed, no distress.

One: **Dosing**–very relaxed, day-dreaming or mind-wandering.

Two: **Relaxed**–at home, on vacation, on a stroll or so forth.

Three: **Normal stress**–pleasantly focused on a task or activity.

Four: **Mild distress**–feeling tension, worry, fear, apprehension, anxiety.

Five: **Mild to moderate distress**–unpleasant feelings but in control.

Six: **Moderate distress**–very unpleasant feelings, able to function but feeling sick to one's stomach or achy.

Seven: **Moderate to high distress**–losing concentration, disrupted breathing, and physical discomfort.

Eight: **High distress**–losing capacity to think, make decisions, problem solve or function physically.

Nine: **High to extreme distress**–thinking is substantially impaired.

Ten: **Extreme distress**–panicked, terror-stricken, non-coherent.

TRACKING How I Feel

Descriptions: Dates:

```
_____  +5—x—x—x—x—x—x—x—x—x—x—x
_____  +4—x—x—x—x—x—x—x—x—x—x—x
_____  +3—x—x—x—x—x—x—x—x—x—x—x
_____  +2—x—x—x—x—x—x—x—x—x—x—x
_____  +1—x—x—x—x—x—x—x—x—x—x—x
_____   0—x—x—x—x—x—x—x—x—x—x—x
_____  -1—x—x—x—x—x—x—x—x—x—x—x
_____  -2—x—x—x—x—x—x—x—x—x—x—x
_____  -3—x—x—x—x—x—x—x—x—x—x—x
_____  -4—x—x—x—x—x—x—x—x—x—x—x
_____  -5—x—x—x—x—x—x—x—x—x—x—x
```

Descriptions: Dates:

```
_____  +5—x—x—x—x—x—x—x—x—x—x—x
_____  +4—x—x—x—x—x—x—x—x—x—x—x
_____  +3—x—x—x—x—x—x—x—x—x—x—x
_____  +2—x—x—x—x—x—x—x—x—x—x—x
_____  +1—x—x—x—x—x—x—x—x—x—x—x
_____   0—x—x—x—x—x—x—x—x—x—x—x
_____  -1—x—x—x—x—x—x—x—x—x—x—x
_____  -2—x—x—x—x—x—x—x—x—x—x—x
_____  -3—x—x—x—x—x—x—x—x—x—x—x
_____  -4—x—x—x—x—x—x—x—x—x—x—x
_____  -5—x—x—x—x—x—x—x—x—x—x—x
```

Feeling Low: sad, anxious, empty, hopeless, pessimistic, guilty, worthless, uninterested, isolated, irregular sleep, irregular eating, fatigue, slow, tired all the time, restless, irritable, difficulty concentrating, difficulty remembering, difficulty making decisions, aches, pains, constipation, thoughts of death or suicide, or attempted suicide.

Feeling High: euphoric, expansive, irritable, invincible, unwarranted optimism, grandiose delusions, hyperactive, excessive plans, participation in numerous activities, flight of ideas, little or no sleep needed, distractible, sudden rage or sudden paranoia.

Balancing: sleep routinely, to bed at the same time, up at the same time, eat well at the same times, drink water, exercise, go outside daily, bathe, be financially responsible, restrict TV watching, meditate, relax, interact socially, have a sense of goal or purpose, simplify lifestyle or goals, get counseling or take medication appropriately.

BALANCING How I Feel

Circle 3-5 priority activities: *routine sleep, eat well, drink water, exercise, go outside, bathe, be financially responsible, restrict TV, meditate, relax, interact socially, have a sense of goal or purpose, simplify lifestyle or goals, get counseling or take medication appropriately.*

Dates:

6am
7am
8am
9am
10am
11am
Noon
1pm
2pm
3pm
4pm
5pm
6pm
7pm
8pm
9pm
10pm
11pm

Dates:

6am
7am
8am
9am
10am
11am
Noon
1pm
2pm
3pm
4pm
5pm
6pm
7pm
8pm
9pm
10pm
11pm

Validity of Cognition (VoC) Scale

Name a specific difficult event: _____

Fact and feeling may differ greatly. Activities to reprocess memory may realign fact and feeling. Rate the following statements based on the most prominent feeling at the moment you are answering, before and after you complete the Stories of Trauma. Try to answer as honestly as possible.

On a scale of 1-7, where 1 is all the way false and 7 is all the way true, circle a number to show how true or false each statement **FEELS**:

Right now, as I think about this event before I do the activities:

It was my fault	FALSE	1	2	3	4	5	6	7	TRUE
I am helpless	FALSE	1	2	3	4	5	6	7	TRUE
I'll never get over it	FALSE	1	2	3	4	5	6	7	TRUE
I'm a good person	FALSE	1	2	3	4	5	6	7	TRUE
I did my best	FALSE	1	2	3	4	5	6	7	TRUE
I'm okay now	FALSE	1	2	3	4	5	6	7	TRUE

Right now, as I think about it after I did the activities:

It was my fault	FALSE	1	2	3	4	5	6	7	TRUE
I am helpless	FALSE	1	2	3	4	5	6	7	TRUE
I'll never get over it	FALSE	1	2	3	4	5	6	7	TRUE
I'm a good person	FALSE	1	2	3	4	5	6	7	TRUE
I did my best	FALSE	1	2	3	4	5	6	7	TRUE
I'm okay now	FALSE	1	2	3	4	5	6	7	TRUE

Reflections:

Shapiro, F. (2001). *Eye movement desensitization and reprocessing: Basic principles, protocols and procedures.* (2nd ed.) New York: Guilford Press.

WORKSHOP EVALUATION REPORT
Alternatives to Violence Project New York Office
Others please keep your local AVP office or AVP/USA informed of workshops.

Area Council _____ Location: _____
Form completed by: _____ Dates: __/__/__ – __/__/__

Language: English _____   Spanish _____   Other: _____
Level *(circle)*:   Level I   Level II   Level T4F
Participants: # Started _____   # Completed _____
Topic of Level II or Advanced: _____

Type of Group
_____ Adult Community:_____
_____ Multigenerational Community:_____
_____ Prison: _____
_____ Youth: _____
_____ Other:_____

Total Workshop Hrs: _____
outside facilitators _____ X Hours _____ = TOTAL _____
inside facilitators   _____ X Hours _____ = TOTAL _____
outside participants _____ X Hours _____ = TOTAL _____
inside participants   _____ X Hours _____ = TOTAL _____

Please calculate the number of hours contributed by facilitators and by participants. Please include in your calculations travel time, prep time, and team building as appropriate.

Please attach a LIST of PARTICIPANTS and FACILITATORS (include DIN or name/address/telephone and note if someone is under the age of 18).

Please comment on anything unique about the workshop (process/team/potential facilitators/new learnings/great experiences).

Please return this form with attached lists and comments to: AVP/NY, PO Box 54, Poplar Ridge, NY 13139 or email to AVPNYSO@aol.com

Readings and Resources

Alternatives to Violence Project
New York State Office: http://www.avpny.org
U.S.A. Office: http://www.avpusa.org
International Office: http://www.avpinternational.org

Co-Counseling
Jackins, Harvey (1981), The art of listening: A talk to the Merced County (California) Mental Health Association, *Present Time 46*, p 48. (see http://www.rc.org / Publications / Index of Articles)

Articles by Katie Kauffman or Caroline New, from http://www.rc.org.

Healing from Trauma
Herman, Judith (1997). *Trauma and recovery: The aftermath of violence–from domestic abuse to political terror.* New York, NY: Basic Books.

Levine, Peter and Ann Frederick (1997). *Waking the tiger: Healing trauma: The innate capacity to transform overwhelming experiences.* Berkeley, CA: North Atlantic Books.

Validity of Cognition (VoC) Scale
Shapiro, F. (2001). *Eye movement desensitization and reprocessing: Basic principles, protocols and procedures.* (2nd ed.) New York, NY: Guilford Press.

Trauma and Community
Bloom, Sandra L. (1997). *Creating sanctuary: Toward the evolution of sane societies.* New York, NY: Routledge.

Self-Medication and Addiction
Guidry, Laurie and Dusty Miller (2001). *Addictions and trauma recovery: Healing the body, mind and spirit.* New York, NY: W.W. Norton.

Dissociation
Vineburg, Jeff (2001). *The significant others' guide to living with dissociative identity disorder.* from http://www.op.net/~jeffv/so1.htm

Secondary Trauma and Compassion Fatigue
Gentry, J. Eric (2002). Compassion fatigue: The crucible of transformation. *The Journal of Trauma Practice.* The Haworth Maltreatment and Trauma Press: an Imprint of The Haworth Press, Inc. Vol. 1, No. 3/4, pp 37-61.

Gentry, J. Eric (taken Nov 2010). Private Professional Consultation Materials, from http://www.compassionunlimited.com/

Somatic Implications of Trauma
Scaer, Robert C. (2001). *The body bears the burden: Trauma, dissociation and disease.* Binghamton, NY: The Hawthorn Press.

Ogden, Pat; Kakuni Minton; and Clare Pain (2006). *Trauma and the body: A sensorimotor approach to psychotherapy.* New York, NY: W.W. Norton & Company, Inc.

Couples
Johnson, Sue (2004). *The practice of emotionally focused couple therapy: Creating connection.* Basic Principles Into Practice Series. New York, NY: Taylor & Francis Books, Inc.

Combat
Grossman, Dave (2009). *On killing: The psychological cost of learning to kill in war and society.* New York, NY: Back Bay Books.

Shay, Jonathan (1994). *Achilles in Vietnam: Combat trauma and the undoing of character.* New York, NY: Scribner.

Shay, Jonathan; Senator John McCain; and Senator Max Cleland (2003). *Odysseus in America: Combat trauma and the trials of homecoming.* New York, NY: Scribner.

O'Brien, Tim (2009). *The things they carried.* NY, NY: First Mariner Books.